Healing:

The Emerging Holistic Paradigm

by

L. Bauer-Freitag

ISBN 1-880710-30-7

Printed in Canada

Cover Art:
"A Magic Moment"
Watercolor by Marilyn Hughey Phillis.

May this book's streamlining effort stimulate cooperation in the scientific, professional, legal and political communities. We can not remain separate communitites if we are to serve humankind. Until open-minded cooperation happens, *none* of us will be a model of wellness in the sense of honesty, openness, congruency, unselfish motivation and *healthy* pride in what we do.

A great many thanks to Sally Culp and Carl Coleman for all their help.

Figures 1, 2, 4 and 5 are by Sally Culp.

Harken!
Lilo Bauer-Freitag
P.O. Box 41927
Fredericksburg, VA
22404

CONTENTS

FIGURES AND TABLES

INTRODUCTION

This book is written for health care practitioners, users of the various forms of therapies and lawmakers alike, amidst the growing awareness that the health care system in America is in need of profound reformation. This needed health care reform consists of much more than the mere passage of a few bills that redistribute expenses, and a few budget cuts here and there. *It must go deeper than money,* and hence the corresponding debate is likely to continue for a while longer. Much of the current literature is evidence of the fact that America is *ripe* for a major paradigm shift with far-reaching effects on how we think and live, individually and collectively. Last but not least, it will affect the role of science and, perhaps, the very way we conduct research.

These are exciting times for original thinkers as well as those who seek and welcome new, original ideas. However, at the same time, we must be aware that the window for such profound change as this book has in mind might be a limited one, constricted by the time it takes for some powerful lobby to take the lead and simply—once again—make decisions *for* us. It is the author's hope that this book may encourage and stimulate self-responsibility in practitioners and clients, for our own lives, health and welfare, to include how we define it and want it to be treated in the future. Such self-responsibility will inevitably require rigorous self-honesty and hence touch on some of our core beliefs and attitudes. There cannot be any taboos, i.e., myths we dare not touch or talk about. Before we can change anything for the better, we must honestly and rigorously *assess what really is* and the many things that aren't quite so, to include topics of religion, medicine, economic power, science and technology, i.e., the very objects of much of our present-day "reality," if not worshipping.

The purpose of such rigorous honesty is to design and develop a new paradigm for life and wellness and, finally, adjust our health care delivery system accordingly, what it will include or exclude, and agreement on who does what and why. As with all paradigms, systems and theories, the question to be answered is not necessarily whether or not a theory is really true. "Theories don't have to be *right,* but they have to be *useful*" (Jessel-Kenyon, 1994), although, if a model or thought system proves infinitely more useful and applicable as the previous one, one *is* permitted to wonder if we may not, simultaneously, have made progress in our eternal quest for truth. The truth will eventually emerge as a result of our untiring application of the trial-and-error-method, observing usefulness and side-effects of our ideas and attitudes. In fact, this is what life is about: A never-ending game of trials and errors, rethinking and redesigning, unburdening ourselves of garbage and then trying anew. Perhaps this is what we could and should be doing with our thoughts, believes and attitudes around our health and health care, triggered by the obvious economic and ethical crisis we are all in: As we are rethinking and redesigning *who* "deserves" health and *how much* of it (in dollar figures), perhaps we could also re-examine just *what* we call health and wellness, or ill health and dis-ease, because, if life is only bearable while consuming enormous amounts of drugs, there is obviously something wrong with what we expect life to be or how we go about it. Also, extending such a life by a few weeks or months, can surely not qualify as "health" care either. We must be careful not to confuse sick care with health care, "Or, as they might say in Washington, it's health, stupid, not sickness" (Green, 1994).

No one argues the enormous medical advances and advantages they bring in regards to acute sick care. However, what about the vast arena of human *self-care,* the essence of disease prevention and alleviation of chronic, debilitating illness? Is there something wrong with our stepping in and assuming self-responsibility, to include the development and acculturation of the vast health-related resources derived from other cultures, for example? I think not. This may be one of the more important moments in our human history, whereby we recognize (via trial and error) the shortcomings and fallacies of expecting salvation from *worldly* institutions (e.g., the medical practitioners and pharmaceutical companies) of the kind that no human being can ever find there. God gives us so much help along our way of self-discovery, self-responsibility and self-care, to include medicines and therapies, worldly and spiritual teachers but, ultimately, we cannot dump the responsibility for our lives, well-being and development on anyone's shoulders but our own. No wonder we feel the medical establishment has let us down: Medicine has claimed and assumed responsibilities and capacities that are impossible to fulfill by any *human* being! What better way to show us our collective erring than the crisis we are currently faced with.

May we rise to the occasion and face this challenge, fair and square and, above all, may we do so in the kindred atmosphere and spirit befitting this occasion: We are in this together and concerned alike. Along these lines, you may expect that this book...

- ...will be blunt. I say it as I see it, without making excuses or sugar-coating anything. So please forgive me if I step on anyone's toes or dearest beliefs. Please note, too, that I make no claims of knowing it all. Each one of us holds a small piece of the total truth-puzzle; if we just all expressed what we see and know and truly listened to each other, perhaps many errors could have been avoided.
- ...is the presentation of a comprehensive, abstract model (in the most practical and simple terms) to be explored and developed further by modern-day scientists and practitioners of *any* kind of health care who are so inclined. It should have implications for all of "healing," conventional or otherwise, as well as being a "Theory of Personality" of use to psychotherapists.
- ...is a framework for integrating the various healing modalities into one comprehensive mold, offering a uniform language and but *one* definition each of wellness, dis-ease and holistic intervention.

May this book inspire some real interest and active participation in formulating the holistic concept and in making it a practical and *legal* reality in the western hemisphere, for the benefit of practitioners and users of the therapies alike.

PART ONE

THE HEALER AS SOCIAL CRITIC

"The therapist who is really interested in helping the individual is forced into social criticism."

Alan Watts

AMAZING CONTRADICTIONS

Many holistic health practitioners who operate from a body/mind/spirit concept of wellness have run into trouble practicing their art—trouble from lawmakers, the medical establishment, "healers" against "healers," and trouble from neighbors, family and the public at large. Last, but not least, the open-minded consumer of our services must be terribly confused at the myriad of different techniques, modalities and concepts of wellness.

When I applied for a zoning permit to practice my art from my home in Virginia, I was not only met with great hostility in my specific neighborhood and resistance from County Supervisors, but I was also accused by other holistic practitioners saying, "How dare you"...go public and attempt to be legal, let alone publicly and proudly defend what I do!? "The system has no place for us... .We are meant to work *behind* the scene...," in the more or less illegal underground, so to speak. To me this sounds like doom. Like any healthy human being, I strive to find meaning in all that I do and to contribute my gifts and talents to my personal and our collective betterment. As a health practitioner, I must *promote and model* healthy self-esteem. I must "Walk the Talk"—which simply cannot be done when I have to conceal or belittle what I do. And you may agree with me that both—pride in our gifts and talents *and* legally practicing them—just *must* be possible, this day and age, in a country like America.

Today, I am still primarily a "healer." All other skills I added to this basic truth, my innate talent, are secondary at best and definitely subordinated to the fact that *I am a healer.* The counseling skills I learned in graduate school made me a better "healer," and not the other way around. Identifying with the "healer" in ourselves is what should motivate us to attend medical or related training, in order to find our specific expertise and niche within *all* that contributes to human wellness. I believe that this is the way it should be for *all* occupations, but especially for the health care professions, i.e., that the inner calling must exist first, before the appropriate teacher or teaching/school will appear. Today, in our society, many seem to expect that the award of an academic title or degree will *magically* mark the onset of healing powers, that is, at the *end* of some *technical* training. This idea represents a contradiction, i.e. to expect a *miracle* from institutions that expressly shun mysticism and miracles. As a continuation of this same, however erroneous idea, we expect all healers to go through some form of formal, recognized training, which poses a problem because so many "schools" have not yet been invented, certainly not as many as there are demonstrated healing gifts and modalities on earth. Many of the insights related to healing are contrived *intuitively,* like all true insight is, including Einstein's. Insight is, in and by itself, a very mystical thing or moment, the famous "Aha!" which has been the topic of much philosophizing, present and past. It has much less to do with formal learning and social conditioning but is, instead, gained by means of prayer, meditation or other rituals aimed at *bypassing thinking* as we normally know it. Einstein was presumed "napping" all the time (Sylvest, V.M., 1992) when, in fact, he must have been meditating if, when he resumed his pen, the ideas literally and effortlessly came pouring out of it. Those, however, who shun the mystical nature of such labels may prefer to call the same thing "being deeply in *thought.*" However, thinking via the three-dimensional, physical brain really has very little to do with it, because *intuitive insight is knowledge gained by other means than logical deduction or through the senses.* Webster (1979) defines intuition as, "The immediate knowing or learning of something without the conscious use of reasoning; instantaneous apprehension." Intuition is thus the most precious asset we human beings have, *innately,* to acquire truth. There are healers who have literally *discovered* healing knowledge and skill, intuitively, merely by getting in touch with the Creator of all things, as Christ did and modeled for us. If this were not possible at all for us normal mortals, then Christ would not have invited us to follow his *example.*

Other insight can be gained by studying other cultures and their approaches. And some of us were lucky to have crossed paths with a wise teacher who accepted us as an apprentice to continue an ancient oral tradition. The fewest of us, however, have received training in our specific healing modality that would qualify as *formal* training, simply because corresponding *formal* schools do not exist. This is true for intuitive, holistic practitioners, as well as conventional health professionals who are meanwhile resorting to complementary therapies, alike. The unconventional, holistic health care arena has simply not yet been formalized.

On the other hand, for those schools already in existence (e.g.,

Barbara Brennan's School of Healing in Long Island, New York; the Clayton Institute of Natural Healing in Alabama, etc.), there is disagreement as to whose piece of paper (diploma, certificate) may be worthwhile, in the eye of critics, the law or medical associations. This would not usually be a problem for the healer, who helps those who can appreciate it, with or without formal recognition. Healers are, by their very nature, not out to impress the world; they help by virtue of their spiritual connectedness which is the basis for intuition, and not by some presumed value of a piece of paper with some print on it. It is, however, a problem for those in our society who believe in worldly credentials of an otherwise unworldly, *divine gift*. As a result, healers in our merely 200-year-old, modern, western society have been vulnerable, like never before in human history, to public ridicule, harassment, being ostracized from professional communities, and to legal problems, if I live in a State within the US where the mere reference to "healing" is illegal by anyone other than the medical establishment. Well, at least no one was burned at the stake lately, a practice which once almost totally eradicated ancient (pagan) healing wisdom in Europe (in the US, it was the near-eradication of Native American Shamanism). However, the way our American laws read today, they really do not preclude yet another witch hunt. It is not illegal to heal, but *saying* that you do *is*. When telling the truth becomes illegal in this country, then this contradiction alone should be of great concern to all of us: Let's make sure that history will not be repeated, by changing these laws!

A world so full of healing nomenclature as ours—"Earth Healing," "Heal your Inner Child," "Heal your relationship," "Healing words," "Heal the Hate," etc.—and bookstores full of healing-related literature, are evidence of a real public interest in some form of relief, not available through conventional methods. It means that we, as a society, are *hurting*, despite or perhaps even *because* of all our modern inventions, technologies, medicines and resulting lifestyles. This demand, need or hurt, however, can not be effectively attended to in the current legal and political (business) environment. On the one hand, I *mu*st use the term "healing" in my advertisements, in order to *communicate* with the public, if all of America refers to holistic practices as "healing" of one form or another. But if I do, then I become subject to persecution. I am refused zoning permits and business licenses, without which I work illegally in that I do not pay all taxes. Or worse, I am investigated by law enforcement agencies who have the power to downright prohibit me from practicing at all, anywhere in the State or even beyond, even if thousands of others do, all across America and the rest of the world, and proudly publish their insights and successes in books sold right around the corner, in a local bookstore.

Of course, I do not *have* to call myself a "healer." Many try to diffuse the issue by resorting to some other, less "threatening" (to whom?) title, e.g., "Transformational," "Synergistic," "Spiritual Response"...Therapist. Unfortunately, this is one of the reasons why there is so much confusing nomenclature in the holistic health arena; each practitioner currently is inventing their very own therapy designation, many of which, however, may actually consist of the same components, elements, knowledge and very similar techniques. Another unfortunate by-product of such diffusing is that it is a dishonest cat and mouse game which violates everything a health practitioner knows about the value of congruency, self-honesty, and personal oneness/wholeness for *healing*. If healing *simply happens*—as was the case countless times as a result of E. Cayce's work (Stearn, J., 1967), to give but one example—and if people begin to heal as a by-product of my work, why beat around the bush? Are healers supposed to apologize and shamefully hide their treatment results? Would we expect this of any other gift and/or occupation? I think not, as this is a most ludicrous thing to ask of anyone. Besides, it is *unhealthy*, as all instilling of dishonesty and shame is.

And then, of course, one could say to leave *all* healing only to currently *recognized* health care professionals—recognized *by whom*, exactly? Judging from the currently very wide public use and acceptance of and demand for more comprehensive, holistic treatment modalities, I should say that "healing" *is* recognized, by a large segment of the American public, only with corresponding laws lagging behind, as usual. And that's what this little book is about: It is an attempt at conceptualizing a new, holistic health paradigm, *including* holistic treatment modalities, and beginning to design appropriate nomenclature and definitions. Because—from a holistic perspective—how can we leave "healing" to persons who received the kind of training, i.e., westerly *scientific* training, that trains all *spirit* (hence, God, by whatever name) right out of the healing process? And then, after we graduate, the law or professional associations come and regulate whatever remaining spirit away, e.g., by committing every practitioner to use only the so-called "traditional" methods, which are only those *currently taught* in academic institutions. To the holistic-minded, this defies every notion of "healing," i.e., to disregard the spirit within all things is, by definition, *not* to *heal*. Plus there is a factor of stagnation built right into this system.

Just how could it happen, how could we collectively *ever* resort to a "science" and consider it "knowledge" or "truth," when forgetting to ask the authority of all that exists, the authority of life itself—GOD? Our western science in its pursuit of truth has missed its very mark by excluding

God, by using every conceivable method *other* than prayer and meditation to seek *God's* wisdom and guidance in this pursuit. It is His secrets that we seek but, by this omission, proclaim that we can learn them without Him. Since this fact is, in and by itself, evidence of man's *self*-will and *self*-rule, such striving is "a fall from grace" and hence doomed to fail somewhere down the line. To think we can truly know anything at all about God's kingdom, *without* Him, is erroneous and a most arrogant assumption. We shall recognize [our errors] by their fruit and, indeed, we have. The deadly results of this pursuit are staring at us from everywhere; we kindly call them unfortunate "side-effects" of otherwise very necessary and good human inventions. By removing God as the authority, science has been rendered an economic commodity, i.e., *business* is what drives our science. We mostly research and develop potentially *marketable* "knowledge"; we no longer seek knowledge for curiosity's sake. Unfortunately, many economic transactions bear a social price tag, called "externalities of business" (Baumol W.J. & Blinder, A.S., 1986) which are the negative side-effects we tolerate as "unavoidable," so long as we don't change direction, or until we destroy ourselves, whichever comes first. Alas, at least we have learned how we do *not* arrive at wisdom and truth, harmony, health and happiness. As every scientist knows, a scientific experiment *not* yielding the desired results, is a finding in and by itself, and as such, our efforts *have* provided us with a worthwhile answer, after all: It is time to change the direction.

It seems particularly crucial to consult *the* authority, God, the "inventor of life," when it comes to life/death matters which include everything pertaining to human wellness and health, or sickness and suffering. We humans do not heal anything. We also do not give, take or even "save" lives. *God does*. This is so because our *physical* existence is not the only *life* there is, and some even argue if physical life is really *living* at all, because it is the very state of existence during which our *spiritual* components are the most *dormant,* i.e., suppressed into the vastly *unconscious* arena. However, even if we *do* accept that a health paradigm which *excludes* the spirit is *fallible* by its very design, we are still left wondering how much of the key ingredient of "healing," the actual healing components—LOVE or "unconditional, positive regard" in psychotherapeutic language (Corsini, R.J. & Wedding, D., 1989), and INTUITION—can be *formally taught,* if at all. Or, perhaps, it is a *personal attribute* which should really be the *prerequisite* to training. I somehow identify with being a healer, probably because I already possess the inherent ability to funnel health-promoting energies from point A to point B, pretty much as the singer was born with a strong, healthy voice with the innate capacity to make harmonious sounds with it. This sequence of events—*first* feeling/identifying with a calling for a role and *then* receiving training—makes infinitely more sense than the other way around, i.e., that I would hope to be able to carry a tune *after* some voice training, even though I never could before. Not that this would be theoretically impossible to achieve, but I don't believe this is how most singers become what they are. Likewise, years of excruciating technical training and practice alone at a piano does not make me a world-class pianist or *artist*. The same applies to training and practice with a scalpel or the application of "facts" from our many data banks. If I do not find the artist within my being, I remain a *technician*. And, while there is nothing wrong with technicians, let us not confuse the two and speak of western medicine as the proprietors of "the healing *arts*" when, in fact, it is vastly not art what we find there. Only intuition can turn a series of techniques into an art form. Besides, who is the "owner" of a particular artistry? Can anyone seriously presume that, "While I am the artist, there can be no other"?

Perhaps this is why so many healers discover their healing ability as a result of suffering and overcoming a debilitating illness (e.g., Louise Hay, author of *You can heal your life* and *Heal your body*). If I can consciously self-heal (please note that the emphasis here is on *consciousness*, willfulness and deliberation. I do not include the body's autonomous functioning, so long as that remains beyond my conscious awareness and control), this in and by itself is evidence of an innate healing capacity, which exists independent from medical schooling, high school diploma or *any* schooling, for that matter. I discover this capacity, hone it, and then share it with others. This is the most normal and benign thing on earth. In fact, in our world of long-living people—medicine *has* succeeded in prolonging the life span—but who suffer untold stresses and debilitating diseases with little hope for relief or cure, I am continually astounded that we do not jump for joy at any new idea or talent that just may help. We eagerly jump at any new "miracle pill" or *physical* invention, and do not hesitate to *ingest* the most gruesome chemicals, but non-invasive (chemical-free and non-surgical) treatment methods are scrutinized and ridiculed. Amazing!

There has been much talk lately, now that some forms of holistic healing have finally been elevated above the mere raising of an eyebrow or a chuckle, of the incredible potential harm that these therapies may do (Herman, R., 1995). However, this is the very beauty of all spiritual therapies, i.e. of healing: *Healing* is the opposite of *harming*, by definition. It is *never* harmful to get in touch with one's spiritual healing capacities and with God. In fact, it is our birthright and goal, consciously or unconsciously. However, those who are temporarily "out of touch," can use a facilitator.

This facilitator, in its mildest form, can be a prayer (one's own or through someone else). In a much more potent form, since coupled with particular techniques/interventions, plus with the personal attributes of the helper, this facilitator is the healer. In ancient times and through the middle ages in Europe, these healers were pagan midwives, "herb ladies" and wise women, later burnt as witches (Armstrong, M., Pettigrew, M.& Read, D., 1993). On our continent, they were shaman medicine men and women (Stolz, A., 1988). Other cultures have their own equivalent folklore medicine, prior to the advent of modern medical advances whose proudest accomplishment lies *not* so much in the successful treatment of so many diseases, but in its diagnostic abilities, *without the reliance on intuition,* and in the treatment of trauma, acute bacterial infections and medical/surgical emergencies (McDowell, B., 1994). This de-emphasis of our intuitive abilities (which is our very access to the divine) is the one single most important reason why not more medical doctors are, in fact, healers today. Without intuition, medicine stops being an art and becomes a mere series of techniques. At the same time, actual healing goes out the window: I.e., a definition of healing *must* involve some statement about long-term freedom from drugs or other life-long "maintenance" therapy, and also about non-recurrence of disease—two conditions at which much of today's medicine consistently fails. However, as long as these two criteria remain unaddressed, no one can speak of *healing,* neither in a physical nor a spiritual sense. Thirdly and most importantly, a viable definition of healing cannot focus on our physical lives alone. What ultimately defines wellness is what is beneficial for that part of our lives that *continues to live,* beyond our physical deaths, i.e., to "save" a physical body or to "remove" a physical ailment, under any and all circumstances, may not be in the best interest of the soul/mind/spirit, even when it can be done. If it were, no child would ever be born with a birth defect, and no accident/illness would ever occur in the first place. There is meaning beyond the physical realm in everything that exists. A holistic definition of healing, therefore, necessarily includes for the healer (preferably, *together* with the client) to gain a sense of or insight into the *plan* a particular spirit has made for itself. Just because temporary alleviation may be possible, this does not mean that it *should* or *must* be done in all cases. Every intervention *not* benefiting "life after life," ultimately will not benefit this current, physical life and hence is unethical, because it violates *spiritual* laws: Such acts do not contribute to the client's wellness, neither subjectively nor objectively; the client's life will not improve, lessons will not be learned, and maladies will recur. If it is not the same illness, then it will be another, which is exactly the state of health care we are collectively in right now. Most certainly, however, it does not suffice to define the "practice of medicine...as the prevention, diagnosis and treatment of human physical or mental ailments, conditions, diseases, pain or infirmities *by any means or method*" (Code of Virginia, 54.1-2900), which are herewith reserved to medical doctors alone, and consist almost exclusively of chemical and physical manipulations of the body. No wonder the American public is dissatisfied, to include a sizable number of healers, with or without training in conventional methods.

I believe that most medical practitioners and other conventional health professionals sincerely wish to be healers. The long list of medical doctors, Ph.D.'s and other "conventionally credentialed" folks in the health care professions, who have ventured into holistic realms of healing upon recognizing the limitations of their profession, would support this assumption (e.g., Andrew Weil, Bernie Siegel, O. Carl Simonton, Elisabeth Kuebler-Ross, Gerald Jampolsky, Joan Borysenko, Marc Micozzi, Dolores Krieger, and many others). However, still more conventional health professionals are not healers, above and beyond their technical skills. They most certainly are not healing, so long as they ignore the spiritual components of wellness and the healing process, i.e., the *source* where all wellness comes from. Without tapping into our own, innate, spiritual healer, any health practitioner is not much more than a technician, *any* technician, and the results are accordingly. The fact that we have gone to throwing out "broken" body parts and replacing them with "new" ones, is the ultimate admission of failure at *healing*. Why else declare an organ as "unfixable"? In the final analysis, there are no *technical* solutions to what is really a *spiritual* problem, to include the admission and acceptance of human powerlessness, as appropriate.

"At a certain depth of specialization the divisions of scientific knowledge begin to run together because they are far enough advanced to see that the world itself runs together, however clear-cut its parts may have seemed to be. Hence the ever-increasing discussion of the need for a 'unified science' and for a descriptive language common to all departments of science. Hence, too, the growing importance of the very science of description, of communication, of the patterns of signs and signals which represents and elucidates the pattern of the world."

Alan Watts

A NEW NOMENCLATURE

In view of the legal environment of healing, i.e., the prohibition of references to healing and medicine without appropriate credentials, it is even more amazing that, somehow, we have come to refer to holistic therapies as "*Alternative Medicine*," while calling the "real" medicine "*traditional.*" Both are misnomers: As stated, what we call "medicine" today has a relatively brief history, whereby this domain was self-created, more or less forcefully, by its practitioners. And it is now jealously guarded by the medical establishment alone. It has little to do with *traditions,* spanning many generations over hundreds or thousands of years. And it did not *naturally* emerge out of our (or any) culture. Instead, it is our *pagan* ancestry that is our *real* traditional medicine. It has always been...*spiritual* and hence *holistic* medicine, combining nature's abundant gifts with knowledge of the realms beyond (some spiritual existence, by whatever name, of life beyond the physical). This has been so through the ages and across all cultures inhabiting this planet and, hence, more honestly deserves the designation "traditional."

The term, "Alternative Medicine," implies a free-standing and independent form of "medicine," used *in lieu of* some other medicine—something that is neither intended by healers nor is it currently legal. No healer would want to work alone when there are blood, internal injuries, broken bones, fever, cardiac arrest or other life-threatening situations involved. Holistic practitioners, more than anyone else, promote *health care as a team approach:* The more input from various practitioners, the better, just so that one *whole* picture of wellness can emerge. Also and again, please note that the law does not permit any reference to medicine by anyone other than the currently prevailing system of health care. In other words, the illegality is already built into the terminology itself, after which point healers who use this terminology will be vulnerable and continuously find themselves on the defense. We cannot "win for losing," so to speak. For the true healer, this situation is unacceptable, and it sabotages the real miracles we might be wringing, *by working together.* Remember: There is no such thing as "medical or technological *miracles*"; *miracles are always spiritual,* in that they are performed (better, channeled) by the spirit within us, the divine origin of humankind.

The term "*Complementary Medicine,*" in my opinion, is equally inappropriate. To complement the current system implies a hierarchy and the continuation of this *dominance,* instead of the necessary, true cooperative spirit. Moreover, it prevents that we see eye-to-eye, with all proper respect each is due, as we begin to talk and work together.

And working together we should. Pitting one against the other, creating frontiers of enemies, or one looking down on another, would go counter anybody's good health. It is incongruent with any concept of healing because it stirs disharmony and stress, and the resulting undesirable emotions of fear, anger or depression. No one is doubting or questioning the real advances and great value of our "predominant system of health care in the US."...for "treating infectious diseases, acute illness and traumatic injuries," plus the advanced technologies used in the *diagnosis* of disorders. It is, however, also no secret that it is "*significantly less effective* in treating chronic diseases such as arthritis, back pain, cardiovascular disease, hypertension, cancer and AIDS" (USUHS, Course Announcement, Academic Year 1995-96), i.e., long-term, degenerative disorders. On the other hand, evidence of the effectiveness of non-medical therapies is mounting, now that we have begun to scientifically research some of the healing phenomena. The time has come to put our knowledge together and to design a new, *jointly used* nomenclature:

> Let us refer to *all* our practices as *therapies,* i.e., conventional and holistic therapies, respectively.

At the same time, the term "healer" will probably disappear. We are all *health practitioners.* Some of us utilize a holistic paradigm of health and wellness for our work, and others do not. But this is what *really* distinguishes us from each other, above all things. Our choice of treatment modality depends on the paradigm we ascribe to, just as psychologists and clinical counselors are choosing from among psychoanalytic, Gestalt, T/A or other techniques, depending on which school of thought (personality theory) they prefer in order to conceptualize a client's situation. Medical doctors may utilize holistic therapies, but one does not *have* to be a physician to use or "invent" them. Let us, finally, no longer prevent our staling data banks of mere bits of information from being enriched and fertilized by some good, old-fashioned *intuition,* because it is intuition that turns data into knowledge or even wisdom, and technology into an art form. Our health care crisis today, more than ever, could surely benefit from an "Aha" or two.

After we agree on the above terms, the need to monopolize or even control denominations like "healing" or "medicine" will disappear. "Medicine" means different things to different people, regardless of the law. To some it refers to pharmaceuticals, whether or not these are prescribed by a physician ("Did you take your medicine today?"); and for the Native American, "medicine power" has always been a completely mystical/spiritual concept, a force which is capable to evoke an effect, even beyond distance and time (Krippner, S., 1994). "Healing" is a completely subjective experience—the experience of the *helee.* Everyone can and hopefully will heal. But the experience is owned by the recipient of our services. The law has not been able to prevent self-healing or so-called "spontaneous remission," nor was it intended to. However, as it currently reads, one may even get into trouble for getting well without *any* intervention! In fact, among generally healthy individuals, healing *usually* occurs *without* facilitators and third-party-interventions. A good immune system, hence the body's ability to fight back and self-heal, is a hallmark of good health. We may recover spontaneously more often than we know, resist and eliminate viruses and injuries before we even become aware of them. Surely, such self-healing can not be considered illegal or unauthorized. It is the very "healing" we want to encourage and see more of, and it is this self-healing in clients that healers, very specifically, want to tap into and facilitate.

Mothers in this country probably have no idea how dangerously they have been living, "practicing medicine without a license" all the time: We run our children's burned fingers under cool water with the assurance that it will stop hurting soon; my mother used to put a piece of candy on top of a fresh bandage with the promise that this "will make it better" (of course, I could only eat the candy after telling her that it was, in fact, much better); not to forget the countless "remedies" for nose bleeds or hiccups! Perhaps no one would dream of carrying a law to such a ridiculous extreme as to accuse a mother of "practicing medicine," but the point is that I doubt that the law would be able to protect her if she were. It does not protect healers who have been accused of similar, non-invasive "wrong doings." To freely allow the use of the term "healing" would put an end to such arbitrary, whimsical accusations, whereby the burden of proof—the proof of innocence—and untold dollars for legal representation always and unfairly rests on the accused.

In summary, (1) The term "medicine" needs no legal protection. Inasmuch as "Pharmaceuticals" are concerned, these are regulated by the FDA. And (2) Neither self-healing nor the facilitation of self-healing require protection by the law. Rather, both need protection *from* the law, which will be comfortably achieved by adopting the terms "Conventional and Holistic Therapies," with appropriate—least restrictive—definitions of both, to *encourage* healing as much as possible. At the end of this book, I have begun a "dictionary" to encourage streamlining our diverging terminology. This is only a beginning, an attempt at designing *one holistic vocabulary,* which is a job no one person can complete. I encourage everyone so inclined to provide input, fast, for the sake of all practitioners, lawmakers and the public alike. Please write to me at P.O. Box 1428, Centreville, VA 20122-8428.

"Natural events do not obey commandments in the same way that human beings obey the law."

Alan Watts

HEALING—A GIFT

It is not in the nature of most healers to be outspoken, make political waves or any waves, publicly defend themselves or their brethren, let alone to fight. Perhaps this is due to the fact that, to do what we do, we must be *introspective*. People who solely orient themselves via the worldly "reality," by means of external *things*, are not likely to be healers. After all, healing consists of the *transcendence* of worldly things, disease and illness being the consequences of living in the physical world. Or, for some, so-called aggressive behavior just does not fit neatly into their spiritual world view, and all healers, invariably, are very spiritual folks. Regrettably, being spiritual is all too often interpreted as a mandate to keep smiling sweetly all the time, the idea that we have to *prove* that we are loving people, and loving people do not get angry. And then, perhaps, it might be *fear* that keeps many in the closet; we have learned to work "under cover," so to speak, to avoid clashing with the vastly non-spiritual, prevailing world view and resulting (nasty) attitudes. Whatever the reason, I believe healers to be among the most non-politically interested and active in this country.

Considering that our nation is undergoing major changes in our health care system while, concurrently, there is a heightened awareness of and demand for holistic therapies among the American public, the time for healers to come out of the closet is *now.* We simply *must* represent ourselves and speak up, whether we want to or not, for the sake of truth and honesty, the furthering of science and the improvement of services to all people, and hence for an increase of love and light in this world. It is, indeed, a very spiritual thing to do, even in the face of difficulties and opposition. Better yet, it is the spiritual thing to do, *just because* there are difficulties, opposition and even plain nastiness. Last but not least, we owe it to our brethren healers who have already, usually out of sight from the general public, been harassed, violated and outlawed. Believe me, when this happens to you and you urgently need support, you *do* wonder where all your loving brothers and sisters are hiding, and whether it is really *love* or, rather, *fear* that keeps them from offering their voice.

The American public is spending billions of dollars annually for so-called alternative health care (better suited, working definitions and nomenclature will be discussed throughout this book). Ever since the publication of these figures, it seems healers have "graduated" from laughing stock to worthy opponents. In other words, if a respectful talk was never possible before between the hard-core scientifically-oriented, and the "soft" intuitive/sensitive (healer), it appears that we have some attention now, beyond mere ridicule or hostility. In our culture, this happens when money is involved. And while our goal must be *optimum help and healing for all people,* such optimum help must not only be inclusive of holistic practices, but it must also be affordable (Redwood, D., 1995). For those who simply shun away from "money talk," I can assure you that we do not have to talk money—money has already talked, and it got us noticed. Medical practitioners have nearly priced themselves out of the market, which is what drove our health care dilemma to the brink. As long as holistic health care remains considerably less expensive to users, as it is right now, it is attractive without any further financial justification, and we can all focus on the "what" and the "how," instead of the "how much."

However, we do have to seriously put our heads and hearts together to define exactly the "What" and the "How"—exactly what does *holistic* mean? What does it mean, "To heal body, mind and spirit"? We know so much about the body, much less about the mind (e.g., *where* is the mind, specifically, in relation to the body? Is it synonymous with "brain"? If not, how does it interact with the brain and the body? Is this interaction exclusively via the brain or, perhaps, not via the brain at all?), and yet less about the elusive "spirit," let alone how these three components interrelate. To further complicate matters (or spirits), we can throw in the environment, lifestyle, a soul, an ego, a personality, a psyche, consciousness, and even some universal energy, Chi, or God! No wonder our medical profession would prefer to reduce our being to its physical manifestations alone. And no wonder the catholic church spun off the medical profession and blessed it as a separate institution, each ministering to its "own" domain, i.e., the spirit and the body, respectively, as separate entities, so that today it seems we cannot put it back together any more. However, there is only *one* health; there has never been more than one health; and there is only *ONE* who defines health—God, by whatever name.

Putting back together those components which naturally gravitate together because they have never really been separate will automatically effect changes in commonly held world views prevalent in the Western hemisphere today. Holistic therapies, like all therapies, work only inasmuch as they are expressions of a *whole* system of thought. The more "whole" (complete and comprehensive) the underlying theoretical system, the better the results and the broader the spectrum of application to *all* people and all woes.

- As Marc Micozzi, M.D., Ph.D., put it, "...There has to be an entire world view behind it [a holistic system] in terms of: Where does health come from? How do I keep it? How do I get well?"..."It goes...beyond lifestyle. It's an issue of philosophy." Further,
- New or unusual techniques are not necessarily holistic or "the alternative..." if "I don't see them as representing alternative systems." They may, "In effect fit with the allopathic model" (Redwood, D., 1995).
- Also, simply combining a variety of disparate treatment methods does not necessarily make the total treatment more *holistic*: "Holism should, in my view, be grounded in a world view, with hypothesis related to evolution, human condition and transcendence. As in any scientific area, this hypothesis can be tested, with an understanding that any 'testing' will reduce holism into convenient parts. Then, we need to assemble such studies in some meta-analytical manner" (Srinivasan, 1993).
- Or, speaking with William H. Dailey, esq. (1994), "Not alternative medicine. Not allopathic, pharmaceutical-based medicine. Progressive medicine—the next step in the evolution of health care on Earth....A wonderful challenge is before us all—to create a new paradigm in wellness. This vision, this energy, can only come from practitioners and patients."

Furthermore, "The time [for this vision] is now because health care reform is happening now" (Dailey, W., 1994). There appears to be a very crucial but also very, very brief window for holistic health practices to be formulated. If this opportunity goes unused, or is not realized quite fast enough, health care reform will be over, reforming hardly more than the allocation of costs for current, conventional services somehow. I see two other possible outcomes, if we holistic health care practitioners do not jump into this game and rise to the occasion, both outcomes being equally undesirable:

> (1) Healing and healers and their holistic practices, now only vaguely tolerated by the law and by organized health care, may be completely and expressly legislated out the door. If this were to happen, then we would deprive our nation and people of a most vital resource, the most natural and hence also least expensive and *least harmful*

resource on earth. An internist at the Menninger Institute in Kansas allegedly said, "We must face the fact. All these drugs are poisons, with some beneficial side effects!" (Cited by: Green. E., 1994). So, isn't it time we look seriously at not only less harmful, but perhaps completely beneficial avenues, without incurring *any* of the externalities we have become so accustomed to, for everything we do?

(2) Another possible outcome is that the medical establishment grabs some of these holistic techniques and incorporates them into their medical practice, and declares them as the *sole* domain and property of medical practitioners. This was the case with acupuncture and homeopathy, while chiropractors started their own "clique" and accreditation program. Make no mistake: The medical establishment *is* seriously thinking about exactly this, especially since the publication of $-related figures for "alternative" health care. Please note the following sub-title of a recently published article: "Evaluation of promising alternative therapies in well-designed clinical trials will most likely result in expanding the options that *physicians* are able to offer their patients, thereby enhancing *conventional medical* practice" (Pavek R.R. & Trachtenberg, A.I., 1995; emphasis by this author).

When this happens, we need to remember that *healing is a gift*. It has more to do with a practitioner's personal attributes and innate talents than with formal education, titles and diplomas. While holistic *techniques* can be taught, they cannot necessarily be duplicated by just anyone with the same results, if the necessary personal attributes, most notably the spiritual development (degree of connectivity with God), are absent or ignored. God has always reserved the right to pick and choose His own messengers for His gifts, regardless of what we and our institutions may want to say about this subject. If conventional health practitioners were to attempt to incorporate some mere techniques into their therapeutic repertoire, my guess is that they would not be doing this for very long. When even the best tool is placed into improper hands, they will not do the job. Frustrated or triumphantly ("See, I *knew* it would not work"), whatever the case may be, they will give up again and return to the previous paradigm (actually, they never left it but merely replaced one technique for another), i.e., back to the one we started out to change. Hence, the net result would be almost the same as if we outlawed all holistic thinking and practicing outright, except it would happen somewhat later.

Therefore, it cannot be overemphasized how important the pooling of our best efforts (intuition, prayers, intellect and skills), is. RIGHT NOW! Shortly after Dr. Wayne B. Jonas took over the Office of Alternative Medicine within the National Institutes of Health (NIH/OAM) as Director, he gave an opening presentation for a Complementary Medicine Seminar Series in Washington, D.C. At that time, he made it very clear that "Alternative/Complementary Medicine is *not*...natural and *not* holistic or wholistic" (1995). In his very excellent speech, he spoke mostly of homeopathy and acupuncture, and of "spiritual therapies" only as a passing remark. He also conceded that, when homeopathy and acupuncture are removed from their original cultural context (paradigm or world view) and incorporated by our western MDs into their repertoire of therapies, that this drastically changes the appearance (and many of the effects) of this therapy. As stated earlier, this happens because we cannot simply replace a body-therapy with some techniques of a spiritual therapy without changing ourselves, our entire world view and hence the paradigm from which we work: If a therapy works *because* it is holistic, removing it from its holistic context and using it *just like* another conventional *technique,* will render this therapy ineffective. To research and use holistic therapies effectively necessitates a major contextual, cognitive shift. It automatically would require us to depart from the western medical paradigm! However—under significant political pressure, I presume—NIH/OAM will not do this. Whatever NIH/OAM currently invests in terms of research and support, it does not go toward truly *holistic health care reform.* This will have to be done by us, the holistic practitioners. OAM, on the other hand, seems to focus on "alternative/complementary" *medicine,* to integrate into the current medical model, without any changes to this model, certain techniques and modalities, that have heretofore been considered "outside the medical mainstream." Looking at this development from a positive perspective, it is good to know "who does what" and that there will be no competing with each other or duplication of efforts.

"The point is not that one stops choosing, but that one chooses in the knowledge that there is really no choice."

Alan Watts

HEALING AND FEMININITY

Recently, I managed to eavesdrop on the following conversation between two ladies who were commenting on their Sunday morning experience: "His sermon was just fantastic...he was speaking to the women and emphasized that we already *are* powerful, that we need no external validation of this. All we have to do is know about this power and live it, by supporting our men in their struggles. Very much like the men in the battlefield who want us to stand up so they can see us cheering them on, giving them hope, strength and inspiration... ."

While it may be commonplace to hear words like these from a male priest, it is much harder to believe that *women* would repeat such phrases with so much admiration and total acceptance. Haven't we demonstrated our loyalty to masculine endeavors quite enough, through many centuries, cheering them on, even when they were killing our own sons and the earth until she can hardly sustain us any more? Our support of masculine striving borders on *enabling,* literally preventing them from learning that there is a *balance* for everything, and that there is more than just "danger everywhere" that must be conquered, mastered and dominated at all cost. The result of our overly masculine orientation—yes, women's, too, if we blindly support every masculine endeavor to *prove* our loyalty, so that we are *lovable* or at least tolerated and not chastised again as so often in our human history—is FEAR. If we think the world a very dangerous place and forget about its nurturing properties, we will eventually turn it into a very dangerous place. Fear always breads more fear, and thinking is doing. Hence we have together turned the world into one huge battlefield, everybody threatening everybody else with ever deadlier weapons, controls, worldly power and rigid systems to maintain this power...no wonder everyone is afraid, not just nations, but on a very individual level, so that many of us feel the need to carry firearms at all times. People today are ready to "shoot at everything that moves," if not literally then at least mentally, i.e., constantly alert and suspicious and ready to lash out. We see it in behaviors while sitting in rush hour traffic every day, in our most casual interactions at the supermarket, in the gym and in our communities. People feel terribly stressed out and are, therefore, tense and extremely aggressive. It takes very little to set anyone off these days. And these are "the fruits" of a world in which the feminine balance is missing.

"Oh, but things are so much better now," I can hear you say. I know many women who are completely convinced that, if they only apply themselves in all the *right ways,* that they are not experiencing *any* discrimination. And the men in the conversations, of course, immediately point to the many women in high-ranking positions in the world of work and the many laws that protect them. So, is woman today "more equal" to man than ever before? Have we made progress toward "equality of the sexes"? I think not, certainly not in a spiritual sense. The polarization between North and South, between countries and within countries, as well as on the individual level—i.e., head versus womb or genitalia—has never been greater. The North is always intellectual, industrialized, "rich" and powerful in a most worldly sense, marked by cold steel, glass and concrete, money, machines and rigid rules. The South, however, is usually financially less advantaged, more agricultural or skilled in crafts, less educated on the average, more mystical, associated with good "country cooking," country smells, stories, song and dance, passion and compassion. For all these qualities, the South is confused with "dirty" elimination organs, shunned, ridiculed or even scorned by many "intellectuals" in the North. Intellect and rationality as a basis for power and hence "value" are northern inventions. Nevertheless, these values are generally accepted everywhere: Those who do not have them do at least aspire or envy them, although the pitiful effects of such one-sided values are meanwhile visible for and endured by everyone today, even by the supporters of this very polarization themselves. To illustrate, one need only look at all the sexual excesses and those who love to hear about them. How easy it is today to associate public figures (usually male) in sexual scandals and, when this happens, the rest of America is mesmerized and lecherously glued to the TV set. If this is not repression of something below the belt, I don't know what it is.

A culture with so much intolerance for natural occurrences like menstrual cramps, menopause, aging, pain (even birthing pains) and death itself, can hardly see itself on the forefront of "equality between the sexes." A culture that has no room for a woman who is unable to attend to her job because she cannot stand on her feet during the first two days of her menstrual cycle, does not value femininity. We hardly make time for childbirth, let alone child rearing. Any symptoms of menopause must be concealed, because menopause (and aging) is shameful and so annoying to witness for the rest of us. A culture which treasures femininity and nature would gladly account for woman's needs as well as for her contributions, just as publicly and vehemently, as is done for man's needs and contributions. More about masculine or feminine-based values and catering to patriarchy in *Bridging the Models*, later in this book.

We have stood in silence, and we have cheered. We showed empathy and compassion and support for everyone but ourselves. Often, we have cried and screamed, and then we fell silent again, because "there was no use." Since we can only *love our neighbor as we can love ourselves,* we have not truly loved and supported this world of ours if we could not stand by our own truth. Furthermore, we have betrayed our children by not modeling for them that the first duty of any human being is to be true to self. Therein lies part of our feminine guilt and our great struggle. The uncontained masculine is a destroyer, spreading fear, terror and aggression. The contained or "tamed" (counterbalanced) masculine, instead, is *playfully* creative, always seeking to experience itself in physical and intellectual ways. As such, it has the capacity to bring much creative activity, vitality, zest, humor and joy into the world. However, intellect, since coupled with the three-dimensional brain, is a *worldly* affair. *Wisdom* and true knowledge, on the other hand, has much more to do with intuition and the *heart* than with the human brain. Femininity, then, is the wisdom aspect of creation, endowed with foresight and a great sense of responsibility (incidentally, *wisdom* is referred to as *feminine* on numerous occasions in the Bible, e.g., in several of the Proverbs: "Forsake *her* not, and *she* shall preserve thee: love her, and she shall keep thee." Proverbs 4:6). When the masculine and feminine are properly balanced, masculine "games" will never go overboard and become so dominant that they are mistaken for reality, let alone the *only* reality. It is, in essence, a less responsible reality, because it is limited by three-dimensionality. For example, the time span for economic planning a man is willing or able to look into the future is a maximum of only 5-10 years; most often it is only *one year,* i.e., the fiscal year. Truly *long range* effects of anything cannot be considered under such circumstances. We often speak of "making a better world for our children," but we hardly ever really estimate the effects of our actions today that far down the line, as our indiscriminate polluting in the past shows real well. If we believe Cornucopian economists that supply and demand shall eventually normalize pollution, well, then we are still not thinking very clearly, certainly not responsibly, in the sense of *long-range* responsibility "for our children."

Perhaps we can compare "masculinity gone awry" to child-like play, the rules for which are continuously invented and changed as the game goes on. If uncontained by other demands necessary for living, continued playing would create unbelievable havoc. The children would destroy the house and, finally, themselves or each other.

In short, excessive masculinity results in excessive aggression and fear of the same. Excessive femininity, not counterbalanced by masculine forces, would result in a lack of vitality and, ultimately, general depression.

What does this mean for us individually and, specifically, for our health reform? This polarization, masculine and feminine, yin and yang, exists within each one of us, man or woman. The extent to which we support—actively or passively—polarization in the world around us is a reflection of our own, inner polarization. Many of today's chronic disorders may be associated with the neglect of one's feminine voices, e.g., there is evidence of increased incidence of breast cancer in nuns (Dahlke, R., 1992). Usually, we do not respond with empathy to such disorders, by attending more to our feminine needs and voices. Instead, our usual response is that we swing the surgical *scalpel* ever more frantically or *fight against* that stupid cancer or pain by ever more *toxic* means. Both responses are masculine: They represent a call for *weapons,* for more activity and *doing,* when *omission* or *avoidance* of an unhealthy situation or behavior would be more effective and appropriate.

Omission of harmful behaviors, however, is seldom viewed as a solution in our culture which is so bent on always *doing something*. First, *we create* the perfect "breeding ground for cancer" (man-made mental, emotional and environmental "stressors"); then we *fight* the cancer by means of more human creations/inventions, and then we will have to fight the side effects of these weapons as well...it is a never-ending cycle of despair and desperation, when it would be so simple to pause for a second and say, "Okay, this creation was a bad one. Let's *undo* it. Let's live without it. It probably was not meant to be." However, America is a place where people want their cake and eat it, too. Along these lines, I do not recall a single news broadcast during the ozone hole alert a few years ago, that suggested or even mentioned the possibility of returning to cars *without* air conditioning. It is as if, once we created something, we are simply unable to let go of it again, even if it kills us.

However, when we do not omit harmful behaviors, we then necessitate the invocation of "more rules," a body for enforcement of these rules, a new breed of lawyers, and so on, to only *delay* the disaster for a little while longer. We all know deep in our hearts that, ultimately, we will have to admit to defeat, that we will not avoid disaster with this attitude.

Measures aimed at *curbing* undesirable behaviors, will only *prolong* the individual and collective suffering. Try to tell an alcoholic or addict to curb his/her appetite for the drug—under great pains this may be possible for a while, until he/she ultimately succumbs to the illness. *Curbing* is never *curing* or *healing*, neither in intent nor in outcome.

With few exceptions, woman has been looking on. She now has two choices: (1) She can participate actively in the same male endeavors, become equally skillful in them and "go for the kill." This is what we have come to erroneously label "equality." Yes, woman is meanwhile welcome to do this—she now has "man's permission" to become just like him—but she does so at a considerable price to herself. This price consists of guilt and anger. She will experience guilt over not fulfilling the counterbalancing function in this world, even though she is the only one who can, and she becomes just as angry and aggressive as man (she also becomes vulnerable to all the disorders previously considered much more prevalent in men). Or (2) She can say, "Enough is enough. I will neither support nor partake in this silly game any longer. It has become stupid and very, very destructive, with no end in sight. Let's return to our senses." She can do so with great compassion and determination—this is where we gain our strength. Considering the stakes, what does it matter if some may confuse our compassion with aggression. The real difference and benefit of compassion is that it is congruent with good health, while aggression is not.

One thing that she probably can not do much longer is to remain a passive bystander. The pain of such resignation and the resulting depression is simply too great. Also great is the pain that the absence of femininity causes others, especially for our children.

The time has come for femininity to return as a treasured life force. The debate over health reform is along these lines, because *healing is the property of the feminine,* born out of our intuitive selves which connects us with God and God's love and hence give access to healing energy. No woman or man with a suppressed femininity will ever heal or cure. This is why, today, there is such a need for compassionate role models and strong promoters of the *feminine,* e.g., Jeanne Achterberg, Marianne Williamson, Clarissa Pinkola Estes, Lynne Morgan, Matthew Fox, and others. Thank you all for your courageous work!

The Aquarian age is an age of returned femininity, in harmony with masculine forces. But until then, because the scales are currently tilted, femininity must fight and *needs the support of men* in doing so. It is *she* who must ride into the battlefield, whereby it would help greatly if she saw *him,* her beloved, standing up in the crowd cheering *her* on. The only time he has ever done this was when she wanted to be like him. Now, however, she needs to be like herself and needs his support, for the sake of *both*, and for the sake of our children. His support of the feminine will, ultimately, set him free, too; it is the only thing that will. It will render him complete and balanced within himself, while restoring external balance and peace. He will no longer have to be stressed out; and he will stop frustrating and angering himself, because he will no longer keep creating his own worst nightmares, which are scaring himself and everybody else to death. This balance simply *is* more important than any worldly riches, power or inventions, plus all the systems necessary to keep these "values" artificially over-important. Achieving this balance is also very, very urgent, in view of increasing hostilities, disasters, illness and pain on this once so beautiful planet.

To set my very own example of "the feminine," I have written and compiled this book primarily from a feminine perspective: It is written from the bottom of my heart, while ignoring many of the (masculine) "scholarly" clichés that usually *must* accompany a good idea before it will be received by our worldly "masters." For example, I have omitted the endless reference list —more people saying the same thing doesn't make the thing truer or righter. I am also deliberately *not* avoiding the first person format—truth is a very personal experience and can only be shared as such (comparing various collections of data from which "one" "may" or "may not" "imply" or "infer" or "deduce" something, is never really knowing anything). Original thought does not require such disguises, decorations and sales techniques. If the absence of such clichés is the reason for rejection, so be it. We are so full of clichés and so starved for original thought, while the clichés themselves prevent and suppress original thought...so this is something that will have to change, too. Femininity has its own, very valid expression and logic (i.e., *common sense*). Since the feminine is a vital part of the thought material contained herein, translating it first into masculine clichés would simply not do it justice. Rather, it would severely take away from it and I would not be demonstrating, by example, what I am trying to teach.

Let me issue a call: *Not* "Women everywhere, awaken," but rather, "Woman *in* everyone, awaken"! Man, too, is inherently powerful. It is time that he focus on his inner strength, rather than the continuous external validation and proof of his power which never seems enough anyway. He requires no more external validation than he has already received, and certainly no more than he is willing to give woman. It is woman who could really use some now.

"The idea of stuff [or matter] expresses no more than the experience of coming to a limit at which our senses or our instruments are not fine enough to make out the pattern."

Alan Watts

BUT WHERE IS THE RESEARCH?

Western science is in trouble, from within and from without. "There is no task more crucial than reassessing the modern mode of inquiry" (Harman, W.W., 1995). The trouble begins with the insistence on a *fixed* scientific paradigm, while all other things are dynamic and changing. We assume a universe of eternally fixed, physical processes which, in turn, cause everything else, including consciousness. "The current paradigm is materialistic in concept by restricting physical effects to physical causes" (McDowell, B., Interview with Andrew Weil, 1994). Presumably, all began with the Big Bang. However, we must also ask, *"Who or What caused the Big Bang itself"*? And then, we must immediately wonder what may have caused the conditions that were the cause for the Big Bang? And so on, and so on. Those scientists who will not stop questioning at some arbitrary point during the inquiry, declaring victory and the phenomenon in question as "explained," will eventually arrive at the conclusion that consciousness is, indeed, also *causal*:

CONSCIOUSNESS IS THE ORIGINAL STATE OF ENERGY WHICH IS A CREATOR, CARRIER AND TRANSMITTER OF INFORMATION TO ALL THAT EXISTS. IT IS THE INTELLIGENCE WHICH IS LIFE ITSELF.

Or:

LIFE=ENERGY=INFORMATION=CONSCIOUSNESS

"In the beginning was the Word, and the Word was with God, and the Word was God" (John 1). The Bible indicates a conscious intentionality from which intelligent, purposive, creative processes originate, *to include the creation of more consciousness*. Hence consciousness can be *both* caused *and* causal. It can simply be or exist, resting within itself, or it can actively create and cause things, as it chooses. To compare this original and originating energy with a *word* is to compare it with *sound,* a certain energy frequency, containing *information* (as all energy does) which can be *heard,* perceived and understood, can be acted upon or can itself cause activity or turbulence of some kind. Perhaps consciousness can be compared with electricity and viewed along the lines of the British astronomer, Arthur Eddington's famous words: "Electrical force is defined as something which causes motion of electrical charge; an electrical charge is something which exerts electric force."

Where do *ideas* come from, including the ideas for posing scientific questions? Science is only as good as the questions it poses, as the saying goes. One result of the extreme sophistication of our modern measuring capabilities seems to be that these highly treasured measuring results (only what's measurable is considered *real*) themselves prove that the scientific parameters are too rigid and narrow and no longer adequate to explain the emerging phenomena. The phenomena, of course, are not new; however, we have previously been unable to observe them. It is not that "Newtonian laws" are suddenly untrue, but only that there is a universe of other, additional rules and laws, e.g., those that govern consciousness itself, far beyond certain physical phenomena and processes. Instead of frantically "accusing" researchers of poor research design and data, when they seem unable to fit their findings into the one-and-only recognized, scientific mold, it is time to *re-assess the mold.* It has become too small. Actually, we could be jumping for joy and excitement at this recognition, as over finding *any* truth. After all, we really do want to know when something is true or not, don't we? Society has tasked our scientists to go and assess the truth. When they dutifully produce their results, they do not deserve to be chastised for them, as Galileo and Copernicus were. We do not have the right to simply *dislike* these results, certainly not on the basis that we just want to continue to believe that *everything* which exists *began* with an *arbitrary,* completely *coincidental* Big Bang. With all the very religious and spiritual folks in Northern America, who devoutly believe in God's word, God-consciousness and His will (intentionality), how is it possible that we so support this rigid, very limiting scientific framework, curtailing the evolution of science itself?

Staying within the physical realm, people create things every day. It all begins with an idea or question. How could we ever doubt that consciousness can be causal? We invent and change rules, constantly. How much more creative must God be, in comparison? So, yes, even the rules governing physical processes can, theoretically, change. If they did, I would want to know: E.g., if all clocks on the surface of this earth suddenly went faster, would we be able to detect this change or even be inclined to examine it? I doubt it. We tend to resist the assessment of changes to what we already believe to know, and we also render ourselves incapable of exploring additional rules and laws, those governing spiritual processes of consciousness, intention, caring and meaning, and of healing. Without it, however, our know-it-all attitude about the role of science is a complete myth or a religion in and by itself, if not an *addiction,* because we continue to uphold it even in the face of evidence to the contrary or adverse consequences of such a belief—an attitude that characterizes any and all addictions. In medicine, one of the adverse consequences is, for example, our inability to heal so many chronic disorders and, above all, our uncertainty whether our many medicines may even contribute to these disorders.

Let me address one other myth. Advertisements like, "Doctors know best" (TV commercial for a magnesium product for overnight relief of constipation), or "They have studies to prove it [that Excedrin works better for headaches than other painkillers]," or "Desenex—the *doctors'* cure," "Now we're listening to our doctors" (whose #1 recommendation is Ensure), etc., circulate in abundance. So many people *believe* in medical research—*proven* means "beyond any reasonable doubt," right? Unfortunately, this incredible trust in medical research is not justified. Western medicine itself does not adhere to the rigorous standards they so vehemently demand from healers, healing and related studies to demonstrate the efficacy of their methods. "Most therapies applied daily in doctors' offices and hospitals throughout the country have never been tested by the scientific method; their efficacy is unknown" (Eabry, S., 1994). Eabry, further, quotes from a study reviewing 4,000 medical papers, most of which were found inadequate concerning scientific reliability, rationale, protocol and the amount and quality of supporting evidence. Another review of research designs in three leading medical journals found only 16 per cent of published articles over a ten-year period as fulfilling the scientific criteria for randomized controlled trials. "Does this not suggest a double standard? The medical profession insists that complimentary medicine can be evaluated only by randomized clinical trials, while it answers its own therapeutic questions through a wide range of study designs (with randomized clinical trials playing a minor role)" (St. George, D., 1994). In short, not only does Western medicine mislead the public concerning their research *evidence,* but it also projects onto "unwanted" branches of science their very own shortcomings in applying the scientific method. The only feasible explanation for both behaviors is the *power/money motive,* i.e., to attain and retain absolute ownership of total medical knowledge. How can we not worship someone who claims to always *know best* and who has powers over life and death, can *save lives* and who, at the same time, protects us from *quacks* who would only toy with our lives?!

Yet another myth is that there is no scientific evidence for non-traditional healing methods. According to Dr. Jonas, Director of NIH/OAM (1995), the most researched areas within alternative/complementary medicine concern homeopathy and acupuncture. This concentration of research focus makes sense when we remember that OAM does not seriously concern itself with spiritual (energy) therapies. Dr. Jonas also says that what's called "alternative" in the West, is often considered "mainstream medicine" in other parts of the world, that the research evidence that *is* available is quite excellent, and that the main reason for the reluctant acceptance of the data in the Western hemisphere is attributable simply to a *lack of popularity*. Here, the study of the "healer phenomenon" is unpopular research, as it once was highly unpopular to research alcoholism. Not many dare write a dissertation in an emotionally-laden, negatively connoted field.

However, even in the field of subtle energies and energy medicine, the research evidence is mounting. The existence of the "healer phenomenon" itself, as it is often called, is probably no longer in question—if you have doubts, please review the studies by Fahrion et al (1994), and Green et al (1993), for example. As of 1991, there were 141 controlled studies, 62 of which showed statistically significant effects at very stringent testing levels (Benor, D.J., 1991). Studies of "psi-healing" were conducted with water, enzymes, yeast cultures, cells in laboratory culture, plants and animals. A series of studies on human subjects involve skin-response, anxiety, skin wound healing, cardiac complications, hypertension, tension headaches and hemoglobin, with demonstrated, significant effects. "Research on therapeutic touch is among the best in the field of energy medicine" (Schneider, C.J., 1994). Many of these articles were rejected by medical mainstream journals, hence were forced to resort to parapsychological journals or publication in European countries (e.g., England). Not only did mainstream journals attempt to suppress these studies, but now this research is chastised for having been printed in "obscure journals" (Jaroff, 1994). This sounds like a most unfair double-bind—we can't win for losing—when it is science' foremost obligation to remain unbiased and to make *all* findings available to the scientific community and the public at large. A similar double-bind exists when the "biomedical establishment demands scientific [healing-related] evidence, which is very expensive...but at the same time to say we shouldn't spend money on creating that scientific evidence."..."The federal government spends over $10 billion a year subsidizing biomedical research in this country, and the sum total of what we've spent on alternative medicine research in all of history is something less than $20 million" (Redwood, D., Interview with Marc Macozzi, 1995).

These are among the reasons why America lags behind the rest of the world in the exploration of healing-related phenomena, and why medical doctors and the public remain so uneducated on *evidence* regarding these phenomena. Every night, as part of "The News," we hear of yet another medical study and its potential implications for our lives (often the opposite findings of what we heard the week or year prior). Why do they usually pertain to pharmaceuticals and lifestyle changes and rarely, if ever, to the demonstrated effects of Therapeutic Touch or other forms of energy healing? For the latter, interested viewers (who already know about these methods and specifically look for information about them) must switch to not so widely available channels, e.g., The Learning Channel, America is Talking, or Mind Extension University, or watch "The Other Side" on NBC, which is probably—once again—labeled a highly "obscure" program by the critics.

Since 1991, some physicists, surgeons, biochemists and representatives of other disciplines have developed and tested measuring technologies so that, today, we are able to make various reliable diagnoses, e.g., from measuring electrical voltage administered via meridian end-points in human subjects (Jessel-Kenyon, J., 1994), or we can measure a DNA winding and unwinding response to subtle energy treatments (Rein, G., 1994). When correlated with certain other data (e.g., heart activity as measured via EKG), we may finally be in a position to operationally define and measure *love* itself, and hence *healing energy!...* This is not to impress or bore anyone with scientific jargon, but simply to indicate that (1) the myth of "no scientific evidence" for the efficacy of healing is completely untrue, and (2) that what seemed impossible to demonstrate or prove yesterday, is today's reality.

Still, it is difficult in the US to obtain doctors' cooperation in carrying out studies (Benor, D.J., 1991) and, of course, funding for research projects. While some feel that it is always the "inventor's" responsibility to provide the proof for their theories, this requirement is totally impractical under the circumstances outlined above. *Healers simply do not have the necessary resources!* Furthermore, please note that the intuitive healer does not need any scientific proof to know that only love heals, love being goal-directed, well-intentioned, empathetic ENERGY, in a very subtle but highly specific energy frequency. This energy frequency has the capacity to "excite" or "soothe" even the smallest cell or organism to vibrate in like frequencies, regardless of how it is transmitted or evoked. When God puts a gift into your heart and says, "Go, my child, and carry this into the world," proving God wrong or right, scientifically or philosophically, will be the furthest thing from your mind. *We* know *that* it works and *when* it works, often even without client feedback. And most of us are satisfied not knowing so many *how's* and *why's*. Healers do, however, recognize that the materialistic mind set is extremely interested in measurable and replicable proof. But then I must also solicit "materialistic" support and that those who so urgently demand scientific evidence help produce it.

Be reminded that the Big Bang theory itself, which we have pretty much adopted as fact, to this day remains but a *theory*. To my knowledge, there have not been any controlled, replicable laboratory experiments which would at least demonstrate the occurrence of a "Mini-Bang," if not a Big Bang, to show that such an event can at all take place, to include how and why. Have we not accepted this theory without ample, *scientific* proof? Of course, I am certain that Big Bangs can occur, simply because everything thinkable does, in fact, occur *somewhere*, if not in the physical reality, then in some other. However, this example alone exemplifies most of the contradictions mentioned earlier: (1) For the Big Bang theory, the kind of proof usually required under the current, rigid scientific parameters, is not likely to be forthcoming. The data explodes current molds; (2) Requiring scientific proof of healing-related theories but not equally of all others, represents the epitome of differential treatment and thus a bias and unfair discrimination *against* healing, which continues even after the healing phenomenon has been well documented! (3) The biggest contradiction, by far, is that of attitude befitting any true scientist: He or she who implies, "We don't *want* [healing] to work," or "We *don't want to know* [if or that we erred]," stops deserving the title!

Two final, frequently voiced arguments *against* healing and healing-related theories deserve mentioning here:

(1) There are those who admit that, yes, theories aimed at explaining healing-related phenomena do exist; however, they then accuse these of *sounding too good to be true* (Grossinger, R., 1995). Dr. Jonas (1995) calls it a "heuristic bias" in research, when we become attached to theories because they sound good, rather than trusting scientific evidence, first and foremost. I would like to ask Dr. Jonas and all those paranoid of *heurism*: Why would a divine system—as a truly *healing* system must be—*not* appear beautiful to us mortals? We can all expect that it can not be anything *but* beautiful. Furthermore, it would seem as *a bias in and by itself*, to reject a system, any system, *only and just because it is beautiful!* No true

scientist can afford to be thus prejudiced. In short, beware of dismissing, or of anyone who is anxious to dismiss, a theory *for its beauty.*

(2) Another complaint about holistic theories and therapies is that their proponents become "energy junkies" (White, J., 1987). Perhaps this is true in some cases, especially as we first stumble upon the fact that *everything* is energy. This recognition can be quite overwhelming and intriguing. However, we are overly fascinated with it when it stops being useful to our understanding and explaining, let alone manipulation of phenomena. In order for theories to be useful, differentiation between various energy frequencies or "densities" is necessary. *This* is where science *can* and *should* appropriately be focused. However, it is generally impossible to avoid talking about energy or energies, when everything that exists is, in fact, energy in one form or another, from very fine or "subtle" to very dense or solid states. More about "energy junkies" will be addressed in the next chapter, "Can Healing Harm"?

In short—without discrediting the real value and meaning that science can add to our lives—the status of science in our day seems to be highly overrated. Especially, our medical research has been placed on much too high a pedestal. Some scientists themselves request revision of the scientific dogmas, while others (especially in medicine) simply ignore them but continue to demand strict adherence from healers. And, even when we do everything *properly,* i.e., according to strictest scientific regimen, how can we be sure that we have posed *the right questions?* The *right* questions are only those, the answers to which will add value and meaning to life. Conversely, answers to all the wrong questions only clutter our data banks and endlessly confuse people, as is the data on all kinds of contradicting dietary and lifestyle recommendations we are being bombarded with. In my opinion, such a mere accumulation of data and, especially, *confusion* are the typical results or "fruit" of a God-less science; as stated earlier, a science which precludes God cannot possibly pose the right or useful questions. If we consider research as "The only source for hope [for cancer-ridden children]," whereby our monetary contributions are declared as "Your gift of *love* and *life*" (TV fund raiser for St. Jude's Hospital),...good heavens, we *are* confused! Make no mistake: God has always had much more to do with giving hope and love, let alone *life,* than any research ever will.

"For an answer which cannot be expressed the question too cannot be expressed. The riddle does not exist."

L. Wittgenstein

CAN HEALING HARM?

By definition, healing is the opposite of harming. Obviously, I cannot vouch for every healer; however, I want to put the potential "harm" into perspective by relating it to any and all potential abuse of gifts and talents. Also, I want to compare it with our response to other known or suspected dangers to our well-being and will address specific warnings and accusations concerning healing.

1. "Fakes" and "Quacks"

Unfortunately, abuse and "fakes" can be found in any occupation. Additionally, even in the absence of abuse, skill levels always differ from person to person, regardless of degrees and professional titles which aim at securing a certain *minimum* level of training and skill only. Not every Ph.D. in English literature is a Shakespeare! Further, professional organizations which exist in abundance, do not *prevent* abuse in *any* profession, but they do make legal recourse a bit easier. No amount of regulations and law enforcement will ever eradicate crime and fraudulent behavior; they are sure to fill our penitentiaries, however.

What turns a skill into abuse is motivation. Nowhere is purity of thought and intention (i.e., a positive, loving outlook toward life and people) as important as in the healing occupations. Without it, healing simply doesn't happen. Bone fractures and skin wounds may mend, but *healing* does not necessarily occur. An unloving (arrogant, aggressive, depressed, etc.) helper, assisting in repairing a certain body part of mine, harms me concurrently in other ways, as all unloving acts and motivations do. *Healing means the removal of obstacles to wellness,* at least, to temporarily set them aside, so that conscious awareness can catch up, so that it can itself create conditions more conducive to wellness, going forward. The prerequisite, then, for any healer is to *sincerely* wish (or pray) the client well, as well as for the client to *sincerely* wish (or pray) him/herself well. None of this happens without a deep concern for human wellness, one's own or someone else's, without any hidden agendas, prejudices, reservations or personal judgments.

As little attention as our society collectively pays to "invisible" processes and events, such as motivation and intention, we usually find it rather difficult to *sense* these. To assess what lies *beyond* any spoken word or overt behavior, we obviously have to use a *sense* beyond those five known ones, i.e., *intuition*. The problem with intuition is twofold: (a) Not only have we vastly lost this sense on a most personal level (for most, it is simply not valued and honed, from early childhood on but, rather, even actively suppressed); and also, (b) It is not considered a crime, in a legal sense, to merely *think* negative thoughts about each other, i.e., to wish (or "pray") someone else un-well. Ill-will, so to speak, falls into one of society's "black holes" or "blind spots." *Because* it is a blind spot, we have a perfect breeding ground for it and, simultaneously, for its denial, as every blind spot is.

Therefore, people's hidden agendas, our un-conscious motives and intentions, most often do not surface until further down the road, when they manifest themselves in visible results and effects or, perhaps, as the *absence* of desired results and effects. All thoughts and emotions, however hidden from ourselves and/or others, will eventually become tangible, if we ignore or are unable to detect their earlier, more subtle "manifestations" or warning signals. Therefore, we can recognize them in hindsight, by the desirable or undesirable results or effects we produce, however inadvertently and unconsciously. KARMA, then, the law of cause and effect in a spiritual sense, is the divine *mechanism by which we learn and develop toward consciousness*. Remember, life (and redemption) is about making the un-conscious conscious, untiringly, through a long series of trials and errors.

Because of our inherent free will, we will never totally prevent people from abusing their gifts and talents, in regards to the helping professions and others, and we will never *make* everybody apply fully what is available to them. After all, helpers, too, continue to learn about themselves, like everybody else, by experiencing their limitations and trying to overcome these. We do this by making conscious choices, experiencing their results/effects and, eventually, by deliberately modifying our choices in the face of personally unpleasant outcomes. It is our obligation and promise to God and to ourselves to continually strive to become more "complete." But, in the final analysis, each is on his/her own: No one other than oneself is responsible for the fulfillment of this implied promise of life or, contrarily, accountable for the lack of striving toward this goal. To this end, no worldly assurances, including laws and the penal system, will guarantee such striving. So, yes, there are always those who are with the program and those who deviate from it to a smaller or larger degree. And, yes, there will always be "healers" who may, in fact, not heal anything, depending on the nature and degree of their extraneous (usually materialistic or otherwise inferior) motivations and intentions. This is most unfortunate in any occupation affecting human lives, but especially in the healing professions which affect lives at the very core, from within, so to speak, where people are most vulnerable and uncertain. Therefore, I am not intending to excuse any such crime; quite to the contrary: Persons who take on such great responsibilities but then violate these, incur much Karma, beyond that of a common thief! However, let us not forget that the same principle is true for medical doctors as well, for any and all helping professions to whom people take their pain, fears, doubts and innermost tenderness. A broken bone is never "just" a bone fracture—there is always the "Why me?" question to be dealt with; confrontation with pain, weakness and human mortality/vulnerability; perhaps there is a sense of betrayal (e.g., "My body is letting me down"); there may be damaging self-messages concerning one's "stupidity," a "victim" stance, guilt concerning family and work; plus dealing with the omission of dear activities or even compulsions. Invariably, while incapacitated, we are confronted with feelings and questions we usually try quite hard to avoid. After all, this is the implied, very reason behind any and all pain and suffering, but most certainly behind any physical illness! In the eyes of a healer, *not* attending to a client's underlying (mental and emotional) vulnerabilities—the actual cause for the accident or illness or, better yet: This *is* the *actual illness*!—is the *real* crime. It is much less the fact that we all make errors of judgment or that our own bodies can fail us, too, as we try to help someone else's. The latter is to be expected as a normal component of life and never-ever a *crime*.

Medical doctors and psychotherapists maintain enormous liability insurance policies, just *because* they know the stakes, i.e., that they are fallible and that our society is litigious. Ultimately, this recognition (or, rather, people's insane desire to scapegoat, blame and sue) has drastically increased the cost of medical care. The liability insurance coverage represents, in and by itself, the admission that, "Yes, we are fallible," and "Yes, there are quacks in our midst, too." There are those who falsify school records, deliberately lie and cheat, *even* in the medical profession.

Again, not attending to people's vulnerabilities and "blind spots" of conscious awareness—the actual malady—is a crime. This includes making "healing" a hobby or compulsion, in and by itself. As "to heal" means a striving for completeness (i.e., complete *consciousness*) and is, as such, the purpose and goal of life, it can and must not *replace* living one's life.

"Healing cannot be *instead of* living" (Grossinger, R., 1995), for obvious reasons. When used as a past time or escape route, it becomes as sickening as any and all escape routes. In fact, it can become an addiction. As always, one shall recognize this by its fruit or outcome: A genuine helper and healer facilitates life, instead of preventing it. This is not done by redefining or ignoring life's problems (e.g., by instilling that, "All is well") but, rather, by pointing to the deeper meaning of everything that happens, i.e., to the meaning *just beneath the very point a particular client is currently able to perceive.*

Lastly, healing is limited by the healer's *and* client's perceptive abilities and/or the *willingness to look and listen,* in order to draw blind spots into conscious awareness.

2. Fear of Known and Unknown Dangers

We often are quick to point to potential dangers of something new which we don't want or, somehow, fear. In a masculine-oriented society (where stamina to defend an idea always seems more important than the inherent value of an idea itself—as in political debates), the best ideas are likely to be nit-picked to death and never seriously considered. A healthy amount of skepticism prevents us from becoming careless. However, are we, as a nation or world, really care-full? Are we equally quick to prevent or react to *known* dangers? Are we not, instead, downright reckless in regards to how we treat our bodies, minds and habitat? Have not scientists and other, highly concerned individuals, been screaming for decades about ozone holes, pesticides, food additives, global warming, ice cap melting and water/air/soil/noise pollution; unmanageable/indestructible amounts of garbage each year; zero plans and no really *safe* methods to entomb nuclear power plants or to dispose of radioactive waste; the eradication of rain forests, fishes and so many plant and animal species whose role for ecosystems, for us and other life forms, we are only beginning to study? Whoever thought to transport oil, radioactive and other highly toxic materials straight across the world, via ship, plane, train or truck, *is* acting *extremely* recklessly! It is reckless because of all the known dangers of these materials and the statistical probability for accidents to happen. There is a standard joke about city kids not knowing where milk comes from ("No, dummy; not from a milk carton or the grocery store")—*just where do people think clean water and air come from?* No, dummy, not from a sewage plant or in-home air filtration system; it comes from clean, *living* bodies of water and from *forests*! And just how did we come up with this Cornucopian idea of never-ending resources (and ever-expanding markets) *on an undeniably very, very finite planet*?

So, yes, it is prudent to not jump too quickly to ever more chemical or technological solutions, for problems we should really be un-creating and, at least, not risk duplicating them. We should also be prudent concerning technologies which simply (allegedly) add *convenience to our lives.* Most so-called *conveniences* come with a very high price tag and risks *for lives,* probably to be paid for by generations to come.

We are constantly meddling with materials and nature systems of checks and balances most of us do not even care to understand. Mme. Curie found out about radiation the hard way. And so it is with many inventions/discoveries, i.e., in hindsight, *after* the damage has been done. As an undergraduate student (during a course in Ecology), I was very surprised to hear that we have yet to study a potential linkage of underground, nuclear testing in one part of the world with earthquakes erupting elsewhere, not too much later! For a people living so negligently, it is simply incomprehensible that we scream so loudly about the dangers of non-technological and non-chemical approaches, *as in healing*!

We teach our kids as early as in college about the dangers of *electromagnetic pollution.* Thereafter, you will not hear much about this any more. As an undergraduate student, I learned that it is known today that we literally radiate ourselves to death, with electricity alone! Those among us who can "see," are continually appalled by the ugly, green-gray/black "auras" surrounding the heavy power cables alongside American streets. The American household constantly keeps the meter running: Several light bulbs, plus two TV's, a radio somewhere; the washing machine *and* dryer, all at the same time; fans and heat pumps running; the computer is never turned off; and then, of course, there is the microwave oven, too... . "In 1984 the United States, with about 5% of the world's population, accounted for 25% of the world's energy consumption. ...India, with about 15% of the world's people, used only about 1.5%... . In 1986 the 241 million Americans used more energy for air conditioning alone than the 1.05 billion Chinese used for all purposes" (Miller Jr., G., 1988).

Electromagnetic radiation is "radiant energy that can move through a vacuum or through space as waves of oscillating electric and magnetic fields" (Miller Jr., G. 1988). Electromagnetic *pollution,* then, is "a disturbance to the natural flow of energy patterns that is detrimental to the continuance of health, vibrant, balanced life" (Davidson, J., 1987). This topic is in need of much greater study and exposure than has happened in the past, because too many people are affected. "Modern man is bombarded by electromagnetic radiation of his own creation...200 million times more than our ancestors took in from the sun and cosmic sources. Our body and biophysical energies are receivers, conductors and transmitters of this electromagnetic pollution" (Davidson, J., 1987).

"Bio-physicists view sub-atomic matter as energy patterns and forces, vibrating at speeds often approaching that of light" (Davidson, J., 1987). In fact, recent bio-photon research revealed that cells in our bodies have the capacity to communicate with each other via bio-photon activity which can be observed as *light* (Institute for Biophysics, Kaiserslautern, Germany). Finally, matter is nothing else *but* energy, more or less loosely or densely held together through "electromagnetic, gravitational and allied fields" (Davidson, J., 1987). Davidson goes on to say that, as molecules and atoms can be changed permanently through radioactive influences, electromagnetic energy, too, affects movement (due to a change in polarities) of energy patterns at sub-atomic levels. During a lecture at the Fourth Annual Conference of ISSSEEM in Boulder, Colorado (1904), Surgeon Julian Jessel-Kenyon reported that, if an electrical current is administered to the body, the body responds to this with an equal amount of electricity *of the opposite polarization.* The next speaker, Glen Rein, a Biochemist, suggests: "Subtle energy in the body is an *intelligence.* ...DNA can *read* this energy. DNA also has superconductivity properties, among others. ...DNA winding and unwinding activity can be influenced by states of consciousness...e.g., through focused intentionality," in a positive sense, as in healing, or negatively, through ill-will, induced by self or others.

Until more is published and accepted about subtle energies and the electromagnetic fields surrounding and permeating all cells and organisms, from infinitely small ones to entire planets and stars, it is wise to heed the warning concerning the risks and dangers of polluting (altering) these fields through excessive exposure to electrical equipment and to, possibly, increase exposure to the positive/healing influences of various energy therapies.

In summary: Many people who vehemently warn of the dangers of unconventional healing methods, themselves do not heed so many warnings of very real and already proven dangers. Further, all healing takes place *exactly* in the aforementioned energy fields: This is where cell information is influenced, i.e., on the level at which these communicate, in a language that they can understand. It is an "energy language," vibrating at the energy frequency of the positive "messages" of love, hope, acceptance, willingness, trust, kindness and goodness. I can hear you object: "But what about a practitioner who does not vibrate in these frequencies"? Well-spoken. Then there will not be a healing influence, of course. However, the same is true for any conventional therapist or medical doctor touching or treating us with less than kind motives, or with any other ill-will our energy fields may be exposed to. Anywhere. Any time.

3. Specific "Accusations" Concerning Healing

In the following, I would like to address specific "Dangers" addressed in an article which appeared in the Washington Post (Herman, R., 1995), *Therapies Outside the Mainstream:*

- Concerning alternative therapies which involve the ingestion of pills and potions:

  "*Not only is their effectiveness untested, the purity of the products and the consistency of the mixtures from one batch to the other is not assured.*"

  "*FDA can only step in after customers have been harmed.*"

  "*Patient protections are not built into official drug trials.*"

  Fine. Let's test them. What are we waiting for?

- Concerning patients who—due to great pain or discomfort or a life-threatening situation—are willing to try most anything:

  "*Offering false hope or steering patients away from effective treatments.*"

  "*The most conspicuous danger is when people with life-threatening conditions, such as cancer, eschew conventional remedies in favor of alternative treatments that promise something they cannot deliver.*"

  "*Nowhere is alternative medicine's promise more harshly criticized than in the field of cancer, where the stakes are so high, and both patients and doctors are often desperate.*"

  "*The National Cancer Institute warns that the use of unconventional methods may result in the loss of valuable time and the opportunity to receive potentially effective therapy and consequently reduce a patient's chances for cure or control of cancer.*"

Healers neither define nor promise treatment "success" as medical doctors do (for whom death is considered a "failure" on behalf of doctors and of treatment). I have read countless advertisements and articles concerning healing and holistic approaches, none of which promised a cure. Holistic practitioners know that wellness is limited by one's willingness and ability to remove blind spots blocking the client's conscious awareness, so that underlying emotional and mental causes/traumata/unhealthy, repetitive patterns can emerge. These causes/patterns, subsequently, can be changed willfully and consciously. Healing, then, consists of the client's re-decision concerning thinking, feeling and behavior patterns (e.g., habituated response patterns to particular stimuli or situations bearing some traumatic memory; or reframing the traumatic memory, healing/forgiving it, if you will)—something that has heretofore been impossible due to the unconscious nature of these processes and causes. This means that great emphasis is placed on human *free will*: Many, if not all, alternative therapies require the client to assume responsibility for their illness and to "take a major role in her own treatment" (Herman, R. 1995). A healer will not promise anything that ultimately depends on the client's willingness to look and listen, as stated earlier, and to make the required lifestyle changes or re-decisions.

Furthermore, healing depends on one's chosen life plan (a superordinate *free will*) which one can view as an agreement or contract between self and God, prior to being born. *There are illnesses and conditions that have been chosen for karmic reasons*. Removing them would interfere with the person's chosen path. A highly intuitive healer can sense this. However, even if he/she doesn't, this will become evident in the client's resistance to treatment. In case of treatment resistance, therefore, we are either experiencing the client's unwillingness to stretch and consciously learn, or their chosen life path of suffering, for whatever karmic reasons. However, we can be sure of the fact that, either way, this result is subject to a client's *free will*.

How the incorporation of this simple insight could change the stress, pressures and treatment approaches within the medical professions! Why is it that, for most chronic, debilitating illness, medicine is vastly ineffective? Particularly when it comes to cancer, medicine itself can *promise* very little. If the underlying causes are not attended to, the cancer will simply and surely resurface elsewhere. How much effort is put into prolonging a sufferer's physical existence at all cost (literally; at great financial expense, too!), putting the patient "through hell before he died" (Colburn, D., 1995), promising (false) hope for outcomes which *medicine* cannot deliver.

Let us remember that *hope* is a spiritual concept: It neither comes from medicine nor healers or particular therapies. It comes from believing in God and, therefore, in "the best possible outcome for me." Regardless of *specifically how* things will turn out, if we entrust their orchestration to God, we can be sure they will be in everybody's best interest. With this hope, we create the optimal treatment conditions and healing environment within, around and for the client. There is no healing agent more potent than a positive outlook (i.e., love and hope)!

- *"The real risk of the alternative therapy movement is not for the patient who has nothing to lose; it's the patient who has a lot to lose, it's the patient for whom medicine does have therapy but she says, 'Medicine will make me feel bad' " (e.g., chemotherapy).*

Obviously, the concern is not for patients who have literally been "given up by medicine." In those cases where medical means still offer promise, healers and medical doctors could come together and work alongside with each other. This would eliminate the entire argument. In all instances and above all, however, homage must be paid to the patient's free choice and will. By now, it is common knowledge that a patient's TRUST in a particular method is at least as important to healing as the method itself (due to the positive outlook such trust facilitates). In fact, this may be why so many placebo-effects occur. Perhaps it is the reason why *any* medicine or treatment works—ever!

My suggestion: If we are so unsure and neither one of us can "promise" anything, let the patient choose and trust that which they can honestly commit their hearts to, one or the other, or several treatments in combination. I do not think, for example, that building up the immune system via vitamins and herbs or concurrent energy therapy (Reiki, Chakra therapy, Bio-Energy, etc.) would interfere with chemotherapy; in fact, it just may reduce the unpleasant side effects of that therapy. Wellness is, ultimately, the patient's responsibility. A patient will never identify with a top-down, no alternative, dictatorially prescribed treatment method and will, therefore, blame all undesirable outcomes on the helper.

- *"Despite the warnings, many patients turn to alternative medicine as a last resort."*

If it's truly a *last resort,* does it matter? Contrarily, since continued physical existence at any price is *not* the goal of holistic practitioners, they can greatly aid in helping clients "clean house," make peace and thus prepare for the "after-life," something medicine consistently prevents when "promising hope" until the end.

"But it is increasingly apparent to psychotherapists that the normal state of consciousness in our culture is both the context and the breeding ground of mental disease. A complex of societies of vast material wealth bent on mutual destruction is anything but a condition of social health."

Alan Watts

ECONOMICS

"America Inc." is an economic system. It is viewed as such by the rest of the world: It provides the standard for gold value, exchange rates and foreign trade; it is a resource for other countries, e.g., through loans and project funding, or as a home for innumerable refugees. Also, our government views itself as an economic enterprise: Note just the "business" terminology used in political debates of *deficit spending, budget cuts,* tax dollar *revenue,* and *allocation of funds* for Medicare and other programs. Despite the fact that this "system" or "company" may be run inefficiently, it is still an economic enterprise within which people (as specific faces, persons or individuals) are, by and large, replaceable or do not really exist. A company run poorly is still...a company, consisting of *positions, responsibilities* (as per *job descriptions*), and of the ever changing *incumbents* of these positions, in search for the optimal power/profit curve.

A few "characters" and personal/criminal investigations or slandering occasionally remind us—or create the illusion—that we are still dealing with *people* somehow. In reality, however, in any economic system, *persons* and even *life* itself are non-entities. People exist only as taxpayers, consumers, employers and employees. They are made tangible by assigning a particular dollar figure to each *role*. Similarly, life exists only as a *resource* (human or non-human), again, with a particular dollar figure attached to it. Both life and people and their creations (which are *commodities* at a particular *price/dollar value*) are regulated—by and large—by supply and demand. The only value thus recognized is...money. If a dollar figure can, for some reason, *not* be assigned to something—if it cannot be bought or sold—*it is worthless* and cannot be dealt with by that system. No wonder then, that nature, rain forests, a bald eagle or particular plant species and numerous human lives are easily sacrificed when regulated by "the law of supply and demand." The EPA standards specify exactly the ratio (or risk factor) of lives we consider still "safe" to sacrifice as an externality of the system, in order to maintain or save that *system* (instead of saving *life*). Naturally, God and spirit inherently are not economically valuable unless, of course, they can somehow be turned into *commodities* or even *consumers* (as for real estate property or as a resource for the collection plate, for example).

Lives thus rendered *life-less* will forever search for some kind of life outside of these prescribed confines. Spirit (and God) will never accept or tolerate when life is rendered value-less. In our culture, this lifeless predicament is deemed vastly unbearable without drugs—prescription drugs, countless over-the-counter drugs, and illicit drugs. Some people develop compulsions of other kinds (shopping, gambling, bingeing, sex...). But, perhaps, the most common compulsion today is the obsession with one's *health*. If we cannot *feel alive*, deep within, at least let's be physically fit and externally "healthy." Unfortunately, few of us feel that such a goal can be accomplished without the help of drugs, from mineral/nutritional supplements to steroids, to muscle relaxers and pain killers for the side effects of exercising too much, to fiber additives and stool softeners, sleeping aids and many, many "perfectly natural," real life substitutes. One of the many *live* things we have sacrificed in the process is, for example, *real food*. In a highly descriptive manner, some products are simply labeled "Free"—free of *nature*. Why list all the substances no longer contained in egg, cheese and sweet products? Exactly what you would naturally expect, especially in sweets and other foods (sugar, fat, etc.), is *no longer in there*! Hence it is "Free." Heaven only knows what is actually *in* the jar, now that the *food* has disappeared from it! To compensate for the missing food, vitamin and other supplements reign supreme: One ad ("The MDR Challenge" with MDR Fitness Tabs) goes so far as to say, "No matter how good your diet is...why take a chance? If you're missing *one* vitamin, it could hurt the quality of your life." They recommend life-long consumption, for around-the-clock "influence" (there is a AM and a PM version of the drug, both "time released")—if it were true that there is *no* diet good enough to optimally support the human species, God would have let these pills grow from bushes or trees!

To expect life from lifeless commodities is nonsensical. *Not* to relate health to being fully alive and to life having value in and by itself, is equally non-sensical. However, let us remember that common sense—being non-tangible, non-tradable because it is *not a commodity*—is not driving any market or economic system. Only money is. Therefore, we must ask, "Who profits"?

Our health care system is a trillion-dollar *industry* of doctors, nurses, hospitals, managed care companies, pharmaceutical giants and allied endeavors. It comprises "nearly one-sixth of the nation's economy" (Califano, J., 1994). Furthermore, America's health care system is the world's "most expensive to administer at an annual cost approaching $200 billion" (Califano, J., 1994). This industry survives and profits from only one thing: "You getting SICK & staying SICK!" (The Fason Foundation, 1995). Hence many have come to refer to our so-called *health* care system as *sick* care: "We're obsessed with the financing and delivery of sick care," i.e., an "after-the-fact system of care... . Doctors have their sights set on sick care for much the same reasons Willie Sutton robbed banks: That's where the money is."...This "Love affair" with sick care has created a "virtually limitless sea of ills and injuries that we can diagnose and treat," very much like a self-fulfilling prophecy: "Concentrating so much of our dollars and brains on extending the life of the near-dead, we have produced a population that, on the whole, is sicker... ." Hence, we are "Keeping sick people alive" instead of "Keeping people healthy in the first place" (Califano, J. 1994).

According to Dr. Wayne B. Jonas (1995), only 10-20% of Americans use conventional medicine at all. The cost for treating this minority amounts to roughly 14% of our GNP! Of this, a high share "is consumed during the final stage of life and, for many, the final days and weeks... ." Still, "Since 1970 health spending has climbed at more than double the pace of inflation-and twelve times the rate of population increase" (Califano, J., 1994). You bet we have a health care crisis! However, thinking of adding a few more controls on doctors' fees and procedures or reshuffling some fund allocations here and there, among the said 10-20% of Americans, is not going to fix anything, is not going to increase access to reasonably priced and effective health care and not expanding the scope of comparably inexpensive preventative and curative methods (to include prayer, touch and simple empathy and personal attention). In fact, it is not going to focus on people's *health* at all. Mr. Califano (former Secretary of Health, Education and Welfare) and many others agree that, for starters, we must take the profit out of sick care.

One of the biggest profiteers of the current system is the pharmaceutical industry (for prescription and non-prescription drugs). It is "The CIA of medical lobbyists...combined with millions of dollars of political contributions" (Califano, J., 1994). Its wealth and resulting influence is so far-reaching that "medical practitioners are educated and pressured, in the intricacies and uses of chemical intervention more by drug companies than by medical schools" (Green, E., 1993). Further, he who profits so well from the results, will gladly shoulder and fund much of our biomedical and pharmaceutical research, of course. According to sound marketing principles—since driven by supply and demand and, therefore, increasing demand or creating new demands wherever possible—this industry will not stop until the market is completely exhausted, until every cell or enzyme or hormone is chemically substituted, regulated or augmented and has thus become marketed. Perhaps this is similar to how the cosmetic industry will not rest until every hair, nail, tooth, cell of the human skin, wrinkled or not, has been attended to and marketed, separately for the skin of the nose, neck or eye, and separately for men, women or even children of various age groups and skin types.... Preferably, we should treat every body part with a variety of products from the minute of birth until burial!

This is not a joke; unfortunately, it is reality—now!—and not just in the cosmetic industry: It has been suggested to screen and treat high school students for signs of hypertension "and 'stepping up' the medication level as necessary—for the rest of their lives" (Green, E., 1993). What an outrageous suggestions, when kids already *snort Ritalin* in our schools for a quick high (Sessions Stepp, L., 1996), quite aside from illicit drugs!

Isn't it time we re-think our drug usage and the example we model on the whole, instead of projecting our collective problem specifically onto the so-called "drug culture," thereby washing our own hands clean of any joint responsibility? In a so-called dysfunctional family," members of this family who actively or passively support the malady of a few, are labeled codependent and enablers. The same is true for any nation or society, and even the human family at large: Has it not occurred to us that *every* member in a dysfunctional society is sick? A culture collectively producing the number of afflicted persons, severity and variety of addictions, is a culture of...ENABLERS! A stand-up comedian summed this up brilliantly during his opening statement on a popular TV evening show: "I'm no longer into drugs; I'm on *medication* now."

How do we collectively enable?

- In general, "We haven't got time for the pain"—a *spiritual* song/message abused to justify the use of pain killers. "Nupe it!" is the same as to say, "Ignore it. Just take Nuprin and keep exercising," despite the warnings your body is giving you.
- "Another Maalox Moment"—Instead of confronting *what* irritates in my life and *why,* we recommend to increase tolerance to irritation by use of a drug (over-the-counter remedy for stomach upsets).

- A Tylenol commercial encourages runners to run after knee surgery, *despite* the pain, simply by numbing it. In fact, the runner who had recent knee surgery, with the help of the drug, runs longer and faster! Is this a healthy recommendation and example of how to treat/use our bodies?
- "The strength of Motrin when your body needs it most"—What this body needs is *not* to walk (the dog) for a while and to reflect upon *why* it is becoming inflexible: Perhaps I *resent* always being the one having to walk the dog? However, Motrin enables me to abuse myself and continue to be used by others, or to avoid making conscious choices.
- "Life is good..." when I can eat what I *want,* healthy or not (Mylanta ad). Similarly, by preventing heartburn from ever starting, Pepcid AC (acid control) enables you to live the life *you* want, and ignore/curtail your natural body feedback.
- "My husband doesn't sleep enough, doesn't eat right...so he takes Megamen. And *he is a better man for it*"—Really? Similarly, can a bran flake breakfast or Tums after a greasy, incapacitating meal forever replace *omitting the harmful behaviors* and replacing them with more appropriate, life-promoting behaviors and attitudes? How many people might actually think of Tums as the only "healthfood" they need, as a result of such advertisement?
- Häagen Dazs promotes addictive behaviors by suggesting we cope with stressful situations by means of food, especially sweets (the kids used sandpaper on the car—"Have a Häagen Dazs"). Similarly, shopping at Pier I..."makes you feel good"—why would anybody actually deal with their problems, in view of so many, much more pleasant escapes?

The list of more or less criminal public messages like the above examples is endless, encouraging drug use to facilitate our living *in spite* of our bodies, nerves and minds, rather than in loving collaboration with them. Some ads even instill *guilt* for suffering pain, rather than offering empathy for its causes and encouraging to look for the same. The important thing is that "the family" does not have to suffer from a moody or otherwise incapacitated Mom: Allegedly, we *owe* it to the people around us to take drugs, because no one wants to know or attend to someone else's pain, and most certainly not to look for any joint responsibility in what causes it! Furthermore, we encourage treating our own reaction to drug addicts in our family/society, again, with drugs, so that we can bear it, without any internal or external changes. This is to make sure that everything and everyone can continue as before, regardless of the effects on self and others. Whenever we do that, we are codependent and enabling, by ensuring that the disease process (individual and collective) *progresses*: Assisted by this neglectful attitude, whatever the illness, it *will* get worse.

"Each day, TV and newspapers report new discoveries and herald cures... . Each night, commercials promise quick relief... . By keeping people alive [and somewhat functioning] without curing the illness [removing causes] or changing their life-styles, they have also helped increase the prevalence of chronic heart disease, etc." (Califano, J., 1994). Advances in treatment have actually enabled people to become and stay sick, by giving "individuals a reason to believe that however they abuse their minds and bodies, science will find a way to repair them" (Califano, J., 1994). No wonder we do not care to make ourselves well, by responsibly removing the causes for disturbances in our lives—or removing ourselves from them—and/or changing to healthier attitudes. Remember: The *attitudinal change* is the actual healing! A new, healthier attitude *precedes any positive changes* we might make in our physical environment or life circumstances! Our own attitudinal change, based on honest self-recognition, is the *prerequisite* for any visible, physically manifested changes, in our bodies or around us!

Therefore, before we scorn or lock up every so-called drug addict in our society, let us look at our own drug use and enabling attitudes/behaviors. Our drug culture is not a coincidence but performs a valuable mirroring-function and lesson: It represents the epitome of many of our culturally condoned but highly contradicting messages, i.e., you are damned if you do [listen to them], and damned if you don't. Perhaps the best example for this is that of a bulimic, who dutifully internalizes and observes all messages of "Consume, consume, consume" and "More is better," on the one hand, but also the current mandate to be fit and trim. I believe this is sufficient incentive to make some of us want to binge and throw up thereafter.

The driving factor *behind* all this nonsense is a trillion-dollar, self-perpetuating industry. Being driven by money instead of common *sense*, it does not *know* how to stop itself. Therefore, "As patients and citizens, you and I have too much at stake to leave driving the health care reform bus to them" (Califano, J., 1994). It is time to "Heal the shame that binds" us (Bradshaw J., 1988) to erroneous decisions, misconceptions and mistakes of the past, by admitting them honestly and then, taking this bus on a new and different road. As we do so, we must, first and foremost, not overly focus on *money* but, rather, on *common sense* and *health*. However, for the money-conscious, it helps to keep in mind that holistic healing methods, *in addition* to standard practices, does not necessarily mean *more* money or *additional* expenses. Holistic approaches might *reduce* health care spending, e.g., by shortening the healing process/time or by attending to actual causes and, thereby, preventing relapse. There are further potential savings in that holistic methods might be suitable to replace standard medical treatments in some cases, or make them altogether unnecessary by recognizing *developing* disorders/problem areas prior to their physical manifestation. If holistic practitioners can provide such services, perhaps the biggest savings yet are in that they charge much less than medical doctors for their services. Such benefits and savings are currently being studied in Germany by insurance carriers, on a several-year trial basis, by simply including *all* services an insured person may choose to correct a health problem as "covered" by the policy. All information—while safeguarding patients' names—is fed into a separate computer program for a variety of specific evaluations. This program is the focus of much public discussion at the moment, during numerous talk shows in Germany (e.g., *Fliege* and *Ilona Christensen*). Rather than waiting for *their* results (in a few years), I believe we must start our own, similar program immediately. However, quite aside from all that, you would think that we would *gladly* pay the price for what really HEALS!

"The rules of communication are not necessarily the rules of the universe, and man is not the role or identity which society thrusts upon him. For when a man no longer confuses himself with the definition of himself that others have given him, he is at once universal and unique. He is universal by virtue of the inseparability of his organism from the cosmos. He is unique in that he is just this organism and not any stereotype of role, class, or identity assumed for the convenience of social communication."

Alan Watts

THE AMERICAN BIAS

As an adolescent growing up in post-war Germany, it irritated me more than once that the more popular movies about Hitler, the Holocaust, Nuremberg trials and the W.W.II era in general originated from *outside* Germany, i.e., American producers and directors. "What arrogance," I used to think. "What gives *them* the idea that they know better than we do what happened *here*"? It took me a long time to detect the German blind spot or bias, due to a shameful denial of our past and errors committed that rendered Germans vastly incapable of objectivity concerning these issues. However, I have also learned that *every* culture has its very own, unique set of biases and blind spots, to include the U.S.A.

Among America's proudest accomplishments is, allegedly, the realization of "Liberty and the Pursuit of Happiness. "American children are taught from early on that theirs is a country of freedom like no other on this planet. America seemingly picked up where European countries have failed. A recent Wal-Mart commercial announces, "We're happy to live in a country where freedom has no bounds." We have unabridged freedom to do ... *what* exactly? As the Catholic priesthood squashed their pagan ancestry in Europe, European "immigrants" squashed Native Americans in the "new world." The first families to become filthy rich in this country, used more than highly dubious methods to get their way—their "freedom" and "success" was acquired on the expense of someone else who wound up having less of the same. From the beginning, this country has been one of violence and survival of the fittest or, rather, the meanest. Today, our children carry guns to school to protect themselves from others' "freedom," because no one else can or would infringe on Americans' much treasured right to be free and to use this freedom as they please, to their individual advantage. Adults carry guns, so children do it, so that, by now, homicide is rapidly becoming one of the leading causes of death by injury.

Whatever happened to the dream? What have we done, or what are we doing today with the freedom we have left? Do we ever stop to take serious inventory, to examine whether our lives match all the lip service we give? Furthermore, when seduced emotionally and brainwashed so early into feeling pride of a thing called "freedom," are we even *capable* to examine it objectively, similar to post-war Germans examining the values and residues of the Third Reich? To an outsider looking in—as any contemporary immigrant—it looks as if there is more crippling *fear* of freedom-*abusers* than any real freedom left with which to do anything. The outsider clearly sees access to freedom rigidly controlled via access to the almighty dollar on the one hand, and through blatant violence on the other. Also, everyone involved learns to glorify this system of imbalance and everything that keeps us fearful and dysfunctional, i.e., un-free. Hence *everyone supports it*—those who benefit from this imbalance (abusers), *and* those who actually suffer from it (victims)! Whenever people support and love what hurts them, completely unknowingly, this qualifies as a blind spot or as "sleeping with the enemy."

When we vote Republican for fear of a tax increase by the Democrats, when we actually favor democratic programs, we inadvertently favor *greed*. For fear of winding up with *even less* freedom (or dollars/power as our ticket to freedom, as we have come to know it), we continuously play into the pockets of freedom-abusers, those who frighten and threaten us. People who love an independent but less popular political candidate often give their vote to one who appears closer to the finishing line, for fear that their votes would be *wasted* on a *loser*! How can investing in someone or something I believe in *ever* be considered a *waste*? If we all had more courage to vote as we truly believe—who knows? Our candidate just might have a chance.

In this fashion—out of *fear,* rather than following the dictates of our hearts—we inadvertently support drug use, ill health, violence, the incredible imbalance between rich and poor in America, continued destruction of our natural habitat and human values. Why? Because human values are *heart*-felt, i.e., they are perceived in the heart, instead of the head, belly or genitals. Whenever we make a choice based on fear, this decision does not originate from the heart—guaranteed! Fear is negative—nothing positive can possibly come out of it in the long run. If more of us went with their heart's desire, we would focus on issues that *really* hurt us and we would be doing something about *those,* regardless of the risk. We would, for example, focus on who we would *truly* like to be, and what we *really* would find much more worthwhile doing, rather than struggling for our every-day, physical existence, selling our souls (hearts and innermost values) while doing so, *plus* feeling absolutely powerless about it: As if we did not have a choice to feel and speak our hearts! But we *do* have to set our fears aside for the moment in order to hear the heart at all. The saying, to "take a heart," as referring to courage and overcoming fear, is no coincidence!

Currently, we have the "freedom" to be physically alive: Living means to make money or feel guilty over not making any or ever enough; to send our kids to college or feel guilty about not being able to; and to finally wither abandoned and shamed by a "forever-young-society" in a nursing home, in great physical and psychological agony, with all kinds of technologies and medicines prolonging this condition. And then we die. Or, as Metthew Fox (1994) puts it: "Middle class people spend their lives getting educated for work or trained for work, working and recovering from work, and raising kids hoping they are going to get some work. And that's about it, folks!"

In between, we have the freedom to fill our time with: Gaining/losing weight, working out or not, but surely feeling guilty about it most of the time; frantically enjoying a lot of sex or forever feeling guilty ("what's wrong with me?"); buying self-help books and feeling appropriately guilty over not reading or applying them; much shopping, and feeling guilty about spending too much every time; watching a lot of TV and videos and, probably, feeling guilty over not doing anything "more worthwhile"... . And then, there are those who say, "What the heck, I don't care any more. If we are blowing it anyway, we might as well have fun going down," leading to doing all sorts of things in excesses, followed by guilt feelings, and then more excesses to forget the guilt, shame and hopelessness. We seem trapped and, in fact, we are, so long as we don't attend to our blind spots.

The little voice in everyone's heart is the only way out of this trap—the memory of and longing for what *could* be: The return to common sense, sanity and, with it, hope for individual and collective wellness. Our blind spots are our vulnerabilities and liabilities, the areas withdrawn from consciousness, breeding ground for all fears and illnesses, because they unconsciously steer us to love or tolerate what hurts us: The drug, an oppressive spouse, violence in the street or in schools, foodless food, a poisonous environment and people, or stress. The only thing we truly will and should ever feel guilty about is when we know we're sleeping with the enemy, but continue to do so. Therefore, beloved America, wake up! Let's put an end to our dangerous love affairs, by taking a sober look at everything we have come to accept as "normal" and "good" and, *especially,* everything that is generally *glorified*:

- Our general attitude of having already found *the best there is* (e.g., freedom, systems, medicine), prevents any real search for viable alternatives. We like to pretend that, basically, *we have already arrived,* and that all we have to do now is *iron out a few flaws*. This attitude prevents any *substantial* criticism or *major overhaul.*
- We glorify "democracy" and "capitalism," as if these were values in and by themselves. Forms of government and economic systems, to include their inventions (e.g., the health care system), are to be *subordinated* to human/spiritual values. They are only meaningful if they support higher-order goals and *never* a value/goal in and by themselves. If they are, they become self-serving, self-perpetuating, and merely support *each other,* even *against* the will of and beyond any real function and meaning for the majority of people.
- Portraying poor general health as a "medical miracle" and the "best medicine in the world" is the same as selling our many insanities (enabling, violence, addictions, etc.) as "normal," or evil as "good," or a lie for "the truth."

I believe we Americans, individually and collectively, have lost a great deal of our capacity to self-criticize and hence to self-correct (i.e., to HEAL). This is a most crucial point in every discussion about health and wellness and at the core of the problem at hand.

PART TWO

THE SOLUTION: HOLISM

"It occurred to us that there must be elements of healing that go beyond technique."

Benjamin Shield & Richard Carlson

COMPARISON OF PREVALENT WESTERN MODELS

The term *Paradigm,* in this book, is used to denote an entire system of thought or world view, as opposed to the term *Model.* Within each paradigm, there can be a vast number of models aiming to conceptualize various different phenomena which all make sense (do not contradict each other or the governing thought system) when re-assembled into their originating paradigm. Each paradigm produces its own philosophical and scientific lines of inquiry (e.g., research questions) which all bear that paradigm's thumb print or signature.

For comparison and contrast (prior to launching into an in-depth discussion of the holistic paradigm/world view) here is a quick overview of models currently in use in our hemisphere to conceptualize health:

A. THE MEDICAL MODEL

1. Major Focus:

In health, the *physical body* is seen as "the total human system." To some minor extent—but definitely in sickness—a vastly undefined and hence elusive "mind" comes into play; i.e., when we are sick, there is suddenly an "I" which wants to view itself as separate from its contemptuous, sick body. If doctors find nothing wrong with the physical body, we then consider "the mind" (whatever and wherever *is* it, in relation to the body and in general?) as sick or malfunctioning.

There is only "sick" and "not sick," whereby sick is *bad,* and not sick is *good.* Illness and death must be avoided at all cost. Please note that there is no real definition of "health"; health, in general, means the absence of sickness, whereby the statistical average determines the norm or standard for what's considered normal and healthy. As our general health declines collectively, this norm is likely to be continuously adjusted downward.

Some "lifestyle" issues are also considered as part of this system, inasmuch as these contribute to our *physical* condition.

2. Role of Matter and Resulting World View:

Matter (including viruses and bacteria, for example) determines life circumstances and conditions. "I"—presumably some conscious fraction of "the mind"—am the victim of my body's whims; in sickness my body becomes my enemy. Nature (or even life itself?) becomes my enemy.

Life is arbitrary, coincidental and inherently unjust. Man and nature become antagonists.

3. Role of Science:

In a frantic attempt, we invent "science" to try to find some orderly behavior of this universe, although we actually believe it to be chaotic.

4. Purpose of Life:

Life must maintain itself at all costs, no matter how chaotic and nonsensical. When we look at life this way (full of *fear* of all of life's "enemies"), this necessarily involves *controlling/dominating* all other powers that be to "guarantee" our physical survival. Unfortunately, in the long run, exactly the opposite is the result, i.e., the destruction of nature, life forms and, ultimately, our own habitat, health and lives. This is the time (at the latest) when we should realize that *man* who views life/natural cycles/death as an enemy, ***has himself become life's enemy*** .

5. Role of God:

This model (and science) presupposes no God and no spirit and, therefore, does not look for it.

6. Who (in the Health Arena) Uses this Model?

This model is the basis for western medicine, nursing, psychiatry and much of psychology as well.

B. THE DEVELOPMENTAL MODEL

1. Major Focus:

The predominant focus is on the "mind" (as vaguely defined as in the medical model); i.e., "I" am a mind which *has* a body.

2. Purpose of Life:

All people are inherently good. Life consists of development toward betterment, on a continuum with no end point, limited only by physical death. At every point during life, there is a theoretical next point and step to yet a higher level of development.

3. Other Components:

This model presupposes free will. At every point of the development, a person can decide to move on or to stagnate. Thereby, development is *good,* and stagnation is *bad.* However, it is each person's own responsibility to make the good and healthy choice.

4. The Role of Science and God:

This model, utilizing the standard scientific method, does not presuppose or look for God/spirit, with the exception of Transpersonal Psychology.

5. Who Uses this Model:

All counselors, social workers and *some* psychologists ascribe to this model.

C. THE HOLISTIC MODEL

1. Major Focus:

The holistic model is essentially a developmental model, except that development is not limited to one's physical existence (or to one lifetime, for that matter).

2. The Role of Spirit and Resulting World View:

"I" am an eternal *spirit* who has a mind/soul and, *sometimes,* also a temporary physical body. *Mind* and *Soul* are synonymous and consist of nothing but interacting, subtle energy fields.

The spirit (a completely intelligent energy force endowed with free will and creative powers—a truly "free spirit," so to speak) is in charge of our lives by deliberately *choosing* and *creating* life circumstances and conditions, including our physical bodies and illnesses, so that the soul/mind can learn.

3. Purpose of Life:

Goal of *all* life (spiritual and physical) is *Redemption,* also referred to by some as "Going Home," "Transcending Matter," and many more descriptions of ever the same thing. This is achieved by learning to *consciously* allow our inherent spirit to take over the reigns of our lives. As our less evolved components (less evolved than the spirit) make this decision, what previously occurred *unconsciously* becomes a *conscious choice* and, thereby, a much more powerful process. Therefore, another way to define the purpose of life is to *make the unconscious conscious.* As body and soul/mind consciously follow the inherent spirit, they are, in turn, elevated in an evolutionary or developmental sense.

4. Definition of Wellness:

Wellness, then, is a measure of *how much spirit reigns* within the spirit/soul-mind/body organism at a particular point in time.

a. On a wellness continuum, anything that strengthens the spirit or facilitates its influence in a person's life is a step toward more wellness and hence *healing*.

b. As an absolute, total wellness is achieved in heaven, but also *when the spirit dominates*, even *while* we are still clothed with this physical body, a limited consciousness, ego, etc. Consciously and willingly subordinating our minds and bodies to spirit, represents the optimal attainable wellness here on earth.

5. Definition and Purpose of Dis-Ease:

It follows that physical illness and pain are indicators that "I have strayed from my self-chosen path," and that I have ignored earlier warning signals (e.g., *mental/emotional* suffering like sadness, mental fatigue or perceived stresses; recurring dreams, thoughts and/or feelings; even recurring happenings—those with similar content—in our lives, are indicators as to our chosen lessons and learning goals for the soul). All physical disorders manifest themselves in our subtle energy fields *first*, with their mental and emotional origins/components. On the physical level, the physical disorder is the last resort for learning and only motivator for a person to still change. Illness and pain thus constitute, more or less, "*unconscious learning*," as previous opportunities to *learn consciously* have been declined by the person.

6. Wellness in the Presence of Dis-Ease and Death:

Wellness, according to the holistic view, can be achieved even *in the presence of certain physical, mental and emotional disorders* (as is, for example, specifically the case with any form of birth defects), simply by recognizing/understanding the purpose and meaning of these disorders for the afflicted person and by helping him/her *making peace with them*. Healing does not mean that all physical woes disappear, although many do, whenever the soul no longer needs the disorder for learning (e.g., for karmic reasons). If disorders are removed or healed *before* appropriate learning has occurred, the practitioner has become an enabler and will incur Karma (become energetically drained and/or fall ill). Therefore, *physical wellness is absolutely secondary to spiritual development*, for any holistic practitioner.

7. Role of God:

Holistic, then, means that we entrust our work to God only ("Thy will—not mine—be done. Always. Amen."), even if this occasionally results in dissatisfied clients because they have not received their expected "miracle cure" without doing the necessary work.

Research, too, is entrusted to God; e.g., research questions can be derived at intuitively, e.g., by means of meditation and dreams.

8. Who Uses this Model?

Anyone who has recognized the truth (depth and breadth) of it and cannot help *but* practice and apply it, despite all unresolved questions concerning legality, and despite potential scorn and ridicule.

"The great mistaken assumption if that healing means a physical change for the better. It is believed that part of the body is healed and part is not, and that we know the difference."

"When the body becomes the major concern of the mind, the mind cannot fulfill its potential."

Hugh Prather

THE HOLISTIC PARADIGM:

BODY-MIND-SPIRIT...
...AND THE ENVIRONMENT

Any concept of human life based on holism encompasses four components. Together, these four components function as *a total system*:

- The physical/chemical body;
- the Mind or Soul, consisting of several interrelated energy fields of differing degrees of density;
- a divine spirit spark (energy in its purest, "original" form), located in the human heart; and
- one's environment in its narrowest and broadest sense, from one's physical home,office or town, to the entire universe. The term "environment" includes subtle energy aspects, e.g., whether or not it is harmonious.

The holistic paradigm is a way of *understanding WHAT we are,* as *living organisms* and, particularly, as *human beings*. We should realize that, in scientific terms, "We know next to nothing as to how living things work" (Dr. Robert O. Becker in *Bio-energy: A Healing Art,* 1992). To understand what we are and how we might work, scientists have looked forever for the smallest physical building block of life or, rather, of life's varying *forms/shapes*. For a long time, it was believed that the atom was this tiniest particle of all things. This belief has been discarded. The ability to split the atom with the subsequent release of enormous energies, marked the advent of new directions in science, concerned with detection, measurement and classification of energy waves/frequencies. Since then, we no longer can uphold the distinction between *dead* or *solid* matter on the one hand, and *living* organisms on the other hand: There is nothing *not* alive, i.e., dead or solid! Nothing lifeless can *exist* or *be*, by definition. Everything moves and vibrates in amazing frequencies, whereby "body," volume or form is created by energy particles holding each other in varying distances, by means of electromagnetic fields. It follows that: "All of matter is electromagnetic, is electric in nature. ...We are electrical beings. There's not a single atom, molecule or cell in our body that isn't an electric entity. We are an electromagnetic cloud" (Dr. Elmer E. Green in *Bio-Energy: A Healing Art*, 1992). We are an accumulation of various, interwoven energy fields, each with differing characteristics. Therefore, it is a good idea to look at life in terms of ENERGY, or better, ENERGIES, with varying vibratory rates or FREQUENCIES. Subsequently, we can also detect energy PATTERNS, i.e., fields or "clouds," with varying degrees of DENSITY, indicating how certain energies may be affecting and relating to each other.

The trouble we may have with this concept is that much of energy is *invisible*. However, we have also gotten quite used to the electric switch, wires and outlets in our homes, and we *know* that electricity exists. We know electricity is real because we can *observe its effects*—all we have to do is touch a *live wire* with wet hands, for example—even if we are not among those experts who know how to actually measure and manipulate it. Similarly, we can sensitize ourselves to the subtle energy currents and fields or "clouds" within and around all things and can—once open-minded to this possibility—very well observe and personally experience their effects.

If it is conceivable that it is *energy* which holds every atom and every cell together (and apart from each other), that it is the very reason we can have, see and feel matter at all, we already have very observable, tangible effects of energy. As a next step, let us consider that "Living organisms are sensitive to magnetic fields; living organisms do produce magnetic fields; electrical currents flow within the living organism, and all of these things are part of the living process" (Dr. Robert O. Becker in *Bio-Energy: A Healing Art*, 1992).To make energy fields tangible or observable, even to those of us who do not engage in scientific studies involving fine measuring devices for electromagnetic currents, please take a wire clothes hanger and try the experiment depicted in Figure 1. You may try this with a large, healthy plant, for example. You should hold the hanger just tight enough so that it doesn't flip-flop arbitrarily in your hand, but also so that you can detect its wanting to move when it does. As you slowly move your arm in one steady, but very gradual motion toward the plant, you *will* observe a distinct movement of the hanger-hook *away* from the plant (animal or human being) at least at two very defined points/distances from the plant.

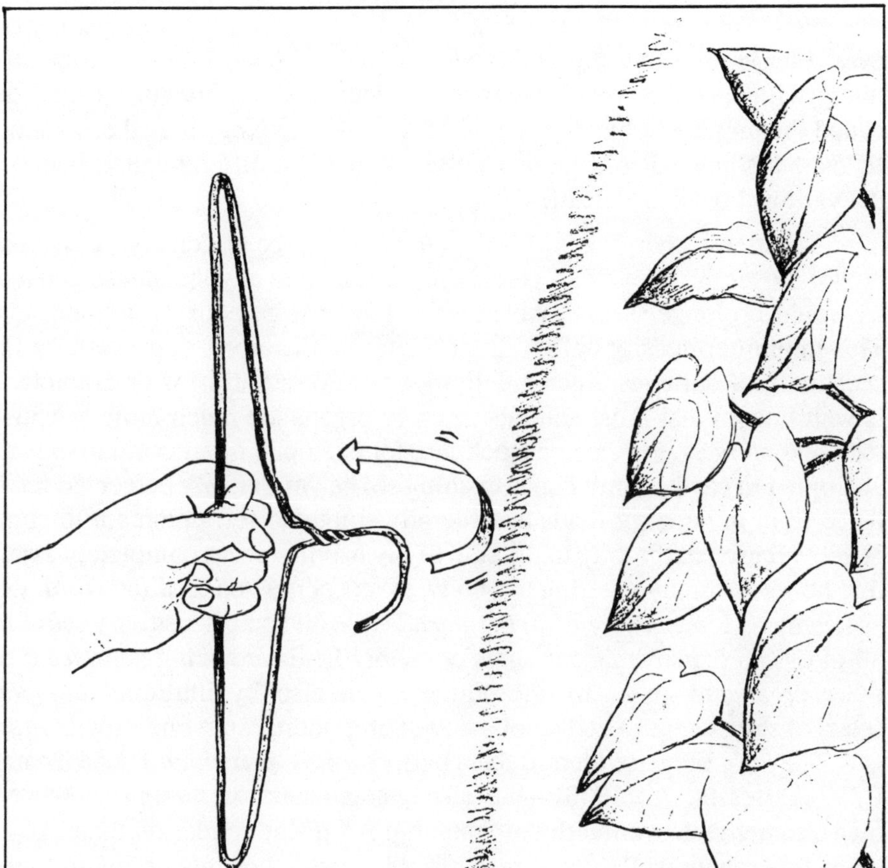

Figure 1: Bio-Energy Bodies of a Plant

These two points correspond to the astral and etheric bio-energy fields of the plant, which will be discussed later in further detail. At this point, you have just experienced two different energy densities—the points where the density *changes*—of two energy fields which are an intrinsic *property* of this plant. They are still part of its *body,* although invisible to most human eyes. Please note that the width and strength of energy fields differ infinitely within and between the species, plant, animal, human, or also so-called "inanimate" objects such as rocks or—*anything*. It is these energy fields that some call AURA or CORONA, without differentiating between the various layers or densities.

Matter is energy at a certain *minimum* degree of density, so that our physical eyes are capable of perceiving it. If it were any less dense, most of us would no longer see it. We would presume it gaseous or non-existent. This minimum-density definition of matter is, therefore, dependent on the sensitivity of our eyes. Such a definition is fairly arbitrary. For example, it is well-known that most animals' sensory organs are much more sensitive than human ones. My late peacock-pet, for example, often came to me and attempted to eat from my hand. In doing so, he very visibly perceived resistance from my energy fields and literally struggled for a moment to come *through* these, all the way to the skin of my hand! He was completely aware that he was actually entering my body, in an energy-sense of the word, just as keenly as I was aware of *being intruded.* With some sensitivity training, all of us can perceive as our auras or energy fields are being penetrated by other organisms (e.g., by mosquitoes), but also by intruding thoughts (glances, for example) and emotions, *not* originating from one's own organism. They not only are identifiable energy *forms*—real *shapes* (Leadbeater, C.W. & Besant, A., 1933)—but also recognizable as *foreign* (not one's own), sometimes even with the "thumbprint" of the sender on them. If we know that sender well, s/he is recognizable by the thoughts or feelings they send our way.

Everyone has experienced being stared at from behind, by somebody else. According to our "normal," western scientific paradigm, this should not be possible: The phenomenon is completely inexplicable because I do not have eyes in the back of my head, and I am not *touched,* in a physical sense. So how can this glance be perceived? Still, everybody *does* perceive it at times, sometimes even coupled with certain emotional reactions, e.g., the hair on the back of the neck standing up, as a signal for discomfort or danger! I am continually amazed that not more people find this phenomenon astonishing enough to research it, just *because* it can not be explained by the prevailing paradigm.

Just as some persons' or animals' sensitivities are *more* developed than others', let us imagine the opposite possibility: If the human, physical eye were any *less* sensitive, we would no longer perceive the physical skin or all flesh at all. We would effectively think that the human body begins and *ends* with its skeletal structure. All we would see is the bones, and we would probably argue if anything else exists at all. Therefore, it is dangerous and *blind* to make our definition of reality contingent upon the sensitivity of our five physical senses: "It is one of the commonest of mistakes to consider that the limit of our power of perception is also the limit of all there is to perceive" (Leadbeater, C.W., 1925). Also, I believe I have sufficiently established—at least empirically—that we not only have and maintain our own bio-energy fields which interact and communicate with each other in some fashion, but that there is additional interchange with energies all around us.

A. BIO-ENERGY FIELDS/BODIES

Let's look at the diagram in Figure 2, depicting the energy fields that are an intricate part of the human body. They are the body's *own* energy fields or *energy bodies*. To distinguish them from environmental, electromagnetic influences, I like to refer to them as *Bio*-Energy fields/bodies: Our *Ether, Astral, Mental* and *Causal Bodies*.

1. The Ether Body, also called the Etheric Double:

The ether body/field has a lot more to do with the physical body than all the other, more subtle energy bodies. It extends but an inch or so above and beyond the physical skin and is vastly colorless. Everyone can readily "see" this *aura*, by unfocusing the eyes somewhat when looking squarely at a person (best visible around the head). It is grayish-white and "shiny"; it seems to be vibrant with light, regardless of the amount of light in the room. We all have experienced seeing the "head next to the head" (slightly moved to one side or the other) as our minds drift. When we quickly blink and all is back in (physical) focus, the ether impression "disappears" from view and we are "paying attention again." In reality, *we are always paying attention and seeing (hearing smelling, etc.) what really is*, if not on the physical level/plane then on some other, subtle energy level. The moment we unfocus from the physical realm, we are immediately tuned in to and completely focused on some other realm, reality or *plane of existence*, as it is often called. This is, for example, the case every night, as the physical brain and sensory equipment "sleeps." However, this insight should also be of serious implications for many psychiatric diagnoses, especially those involving so-called delusions and "hallucinations": Nothing can be

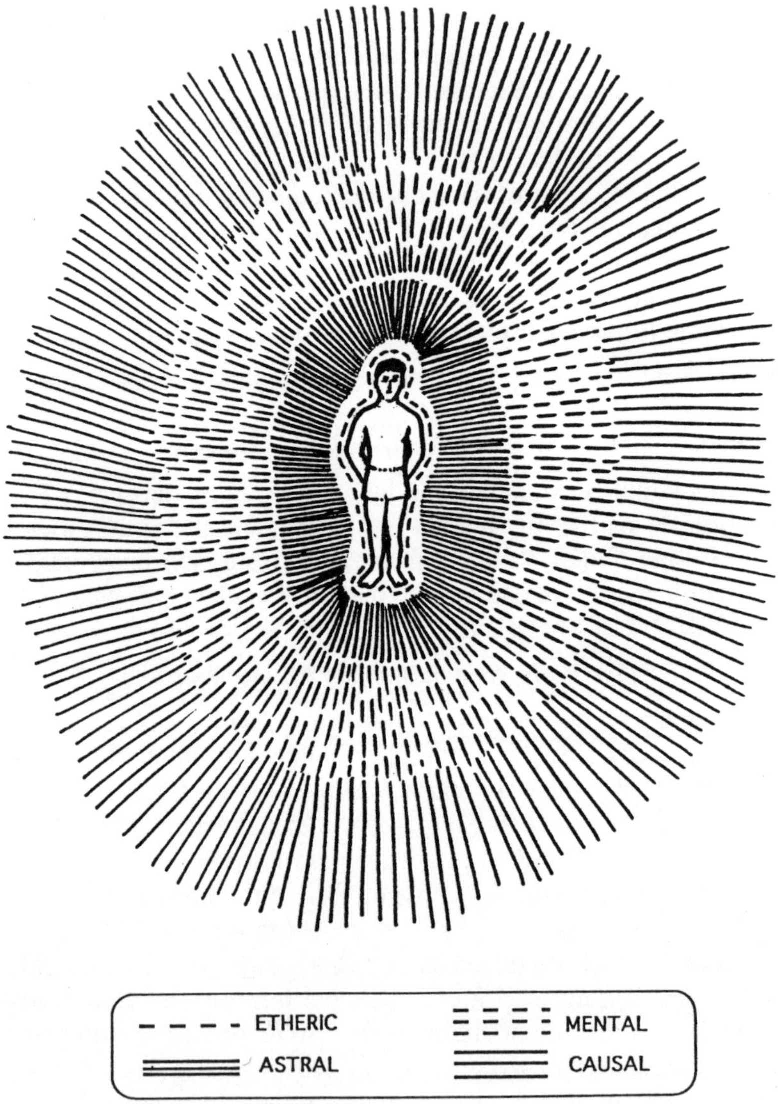

Figure 2: Human Bio-Energy Fields

perceived that does not exist, that is not real on *some* plane of existence. The more skillful "sensitives" among us are capable to tune in *and out* (!), to and from the various planes, *at will* and completely conscious, without risking their sanity.

The ether body is conceptually still a part of the physical body, for the following reasons:

- It is the only energy body that is a perfect replica of the physical body, including all "organs" (in a subtle energy form), "nerves" (meridians)...EVERYTHING. Actually, the physical body is the replica of the ether body—it *follows* the etheric information/consciousness/instructions. The ether body is a "blueprint" of everything that manifests itself physically. It is created *before* the physical body in the womb, and it still exists unharmed, in its entirety, even *after* physical organs or limbs have been surgically removed. This has been demonstrated by means of particularly sensitive photographic processes. The well-known "Phantom Leaf" experiments, for example, show that the etheric leaf can still be photographed in its entirety for some time *after* the physical leaf has been *cut in half*! For the human body, the analogous process may explain the "phantom pain" so frequently reported after amputations. Perhaps, one day, we will be able to draw upon the information contained in the ether aura for the physical body, to actually recreate limbs and organs. It can be presumed that, intuitively, healers already draw upon that information to some extent, when assisting the physical body to restore itself according to its more complete, etheric "blueprint." Most certainly, all self-healing occurs this way (e.g., skin wound healing), human or non-human (e.g., also of animals who are known to recreate lost limbs and body parts).
- The ether body decays/dissolves some time after a person's physical death. The other, more subtle energy bodies live on. Some sensitive people can perceive the etheric double above or near grave sites of recently buried corpses—the basis for a great many ghost stories or "eerie feelings" in grave yards some people experience.
- The ether body is considerably more dense (energetically) than all other energy bodies.
- Unlike the other energy bodies, the etheric double follows the contours and shape of the physical body. The astral, mental and causal bodies are more or less egg-shaped and can be quite large. Furthermore, the latter ones are quite colorful, as opposed to the grayish-white ether aura.

Kirlian photography and sensitive healers can detect (i.e., visually, through "touch" or intuitive "knowing") a person's vitality (life-energy; degree of general health and self-healing capacity at the moment), in general and by region, e.g., in the vicinity of malfunctioning organs. Furthermore, this energetic vitality defect is detectable *before* actual physical symptoms develop or become a serious problem. Scientifically, examining healers' perceptions by following them up with appropriate medical tests, might greatly enhance our collective ability for *early detection* and *prevention* of physical illness.

Everybody has an etheric representation. Incidentally, the ether realm is also the "home" of often-described elves, fairies, etc. These are etheric entities/energy beings endowed with their own consciousness, prior to assuming human form, by way of a human incarnation. Also, humans get "stuck" there sometimes after physical death—their ether body, for some reason, does not dissolve—apparently those not even realizing that they have, in fact, abandoned physical life, e.g., after a suicide attempt. These are people who, due to a perceived attachment to something physical—a loved one, material possessions, etc.—*actually remain physically attached.* Presumably, this is also the realm of so-called *alien encounters*: Please note the subjectively uncomfortable state of being *in-between* and physically *paralyzed* that W. Strieber (1988) and many abductees describe during their encounters: Evidently, children still "switch" from the physical to the etheric energy frequencies with relative ease; but for the adult consciousness, the ether plane is a somewhat uncomfortable reality. Occasionally, as our consciousness returns from a voyage through the existential planes (which *always* includes the etheric field as well), we sometimes get stopped there for a while: There are entire cities with people busily running about; everything is grayish colorless; one cannot really see too well (which is highly uncomfortable); and people appear much taller than one perceives the self... At least, this is how I have sometimes encountered the ether plane.

2. The Astral Body

The astral body represents the *house for our feelings*—all our emotions, conscious and unconscious. It is the most colorful of all energy bodies, containing colors of the entire spectrum of the rainbow. It is in constant motion: Colors change as we think, feel and do things, awake or asleep and dreaming. Its energy frequency (vibratory rate) is higher than that of the ether body, hence it is more subtle and less dense than the physical realm with its etheric component. Further, it is egg-shaped and extends beyond the ether body.

Famous clairvoyants (e.g., C.W. Leadbeater or Dora van Gelder-Kunz) have attempted to capture the color quality of that plane but consistently complained that there is no paint or color on earth that comes even close to the brilliance and radiance of colors as seen astrally. Unfortunately, we can only *describe* the richness, depth and iridescent quality of astral colors. Astral colors are not merely viewed or seen—they are *experienced* with one's entire being! It is impossible to remain *objective* to or with them! Everyone who has ever consciously undertaken an astral voyage will attest to the immense feeling quality inherent in every step or encounter. One can not help but to pause, again and again, while thinking or saying, "Wow!" (incidentally, thinking and saying is the same thing on that plane). At the same time, one has the sensation of some exhilaration similar to that of rapid heartbeat and accelerated breathing.

One of the better depictions of the astral sphere I have ever seen is contained toward the tail end of the Scorsese motion picture, *The Last Temptation of Christ.* After Christ is crucified, yet before he physically expires, he goes on an astral voyage and experiences *what would have been* had he followed his more earthbound feelings, longings and desires (e.g., to marry Magdalene), rather than following the will of the spirit within him. According to Scorsese, there was still enough of those desires in him to prompt this astral voyage, representing his final struggle and subsequent decision, which had to be *100% one way or the other,* on *all* planes of existence. While Scorsese restricted his portrayal of Christ's internal struggles and decisions to the astral realm, we really have to fight "our demons" on *all* existential planes.

Of course, there are *many* artists, foremost painters, who are quite familiar with the astral plane, saw and painted it all the time, e.g., Van Gogh, Gaugin or Cezanne.

All feelings (as well as thoughts) are ENERGY: It takes energy to produce an emotion as it does to shape a thought. Neither will be destroyed but merely transmuted from one form to another. The energy is "packaged" into a particular density (on the astral plane this would be in the form of a feeling quality, color, sound or smell) and then *sent,* either into the environment, to a particular recipient, an object of interest or desire or, if withheld, to some region within ones own bio-energy system. *Sending* means that it has a direction, based on the underlying motivation, hence the energy is goal-directed. Astrally, we can detect motivations and goal-directed activity/turbulence which usually *hide behind* a spoken word or observable deed; e.g., a mother can pick up her screaming baby in a loving way or angrily. Both can be seen in her astral aura by means of color and motion in the aura, or it can be *sensed* if one stands close enough to her. It is not possible to keep many secrets on the astral plane! The baby can definitely feel (see or smell?) the difference. We know, for example, that *fear* has a particular odor and that, at least, *dogs* can smell it, whether we already perspire or not. Perhaps a dog or baby can actually *see* the bluish specks and freckles covering the astral body of a frightened person. In general, it can be said that we—as well as animals and plants—can *sense* when we are in the presence of a happy or unhappy person, regardless of how hard they try to act and behave and control their facial expressions and words, to create a contrary impression.

Just as there are harmonious or disharmonious and health-promoting or unhealthy thoughts, the same is true for emotions. The healer can detect—either visually, through sensing/feeling or by intuitively *knowing*—where in a body feeling energy is concentrated, as well as the nature and quality of these feelings. Flooding the organism with optimism (hope), joy and loving feelings will enhance the person's overall vitality and nourishes it with healthy colors and light. Angry and fearful feelings, on the other hand, literally choke off the light and life, usually in certain areas highly specific to that person and the object of interest or desire. A generalized fear, for example, can constrict energy flow in the area of the throat/neck; more specific fear, e.g., of doing something or taking an important step in a new direction, can block energy in a wrist or arm, or an ankle or leg. Fear involving one's self-esteem (e.g., shame) usually afflicts a person's stomach area; fear of saying something can affect the mouth and lips. For a more detailed description of where in one's bio-energy system both thoughts and emotions affect one's physical well-being, please see L. Hay's book, *Heal your body: The mental causes for physical illness and the metaphysical way to overcome them* (1982), and also T. Dethlefsen & R. Dahlke, *The healing power of illness* (1983).

A commonly experienced "astral pain" is that of a hangover headache, when we say that our head hurts "*...way out there*" or that even the "tip of every hair hurts." This is because alcohol directs energy to areas below the waist (this is also a reason why many people become promiscuous under the influence of alcohol), whereby the upper half is vastly undernourished. Since the modern, western person perceives him/herself mostly as "a head," this is where we are most likely to painfully notice the energy disparity. In reality, however, it might also be noticeable in the heart area or in general, everywhere above the waist. Additionally, many aches and pains we take to physicians for which no physical cause can be found, are actually located in the astral body. We then try to ignore the perception, because there is no name or label for it. Still, experiencing our outer bodies is much more common than might be assumed.

The influence of persistent negative emotions on our physical well-being takes place *through* the ether body. In other words, energy changes are effected in a *trickle-down* fashion or, better, an *inward* fashion, from the less dense to denser bodies. They first affect the astral body in certain regions, then the ether body, *before* effecting any physical changes. The disturbance is detectable and treatable on both of these energy levels for some time, prior to finally manifesting any physical symptoms, thus allowing more time and opportunity for detection, prevention or correction.

Correction at the astral level takes place by flooding the organism or constricted areas with unconditional, positive regard (i.e., *love*), or with specific, healthful colors conducive for the functioning of a particular, afflicted organ, or also with harmonious sounds/music. Drawing on this knowledge, color and music therapies have developed. Therapy using gem stones, utilizing the particular energy quality captured in each (nature of the stone, density and color) is also important to mention here, as well as movement therapies (Tai Chi, dance, etc.) and aroma therapy.

Some plant essences *directly* affect feeling and thinking (astral and mental) bodies (e.g., *Bach Flower Remedies* and perhaps others). Although they are usually ingested orally, they do not cause any chemical changes in the body; that is, not until the body experiences the *trickle-down* effect of what constitutes *unconscious learning,* through the astral and ether auras. Finally, *healing* is experienced in a host of such vague but common physical symptoms, e.g., a runny nose, diarrhea attack or fever. Thereafter, people often feel "brand-new" and are capable to suddenly respond to certain life tasks quite differently than before, much to their own amazement. For more information, please read, *The Bach Flower Remedies* (Bach, E. and Wheeler, F.J., 1977).

It is important that the organism be fed what it is currently unable to give itself, for whatever reason. However, eventually—for any lasting stabilization—one must probe into the person's feeling life and make the causing processes conscious, if they are unconscious, or to find ways that alleviate the underlying unhealthy cravings or emotions. This can be done, for example, by avoiding certain situations or people, once these have been identified, or by creating opportunities for more healthy experiences in one's life.

Self-correction/self-healing is always possible. If we can constrict or *block* our energy flow, all by ourselves, it is self-understood that, at least theoretically, we can also *unblock* ourselves. Ideally, this should always be the case and is done, for example, by touching our aching foot and simply *loving it,* by visualizing sending light into the afflicted regions, and by thinking about causative feeling patterns (e.g., *asking* the foot in one's mind what it needs and what it is rebelling against). In any case, *supplying pain with love is always a very safe bet and good solution! Love never hurts anything or anybody!*

Man-made objects, as well as certain places, can have astral auras or fields, too, i.e., emotional qualities *they are endowed with by human beings,* their makers' or users' imaginations, desires or other emotional affiliations. Oftentimes I have noticed a bright pink, red or purple car passing me by on the road, which was in the physical reality not pink, red or purple at all (one blink of the eye and the color was gone again). I have no idea what this means, except that, perhaps, the owner might wish and desire a bright car but does not dare in "the real world." Or, perhaps, to him/her the car represents exactly such a bright, emotional object: The color may represent the "love affair" some people have with their cars.

There are places famous (or infamous) for their particular feeling quality, e.g., old battlefields (remember General Patton's remarks in the motion picture, *Patton,* as he arrived in Africa and recognized the place of the battlefield he had been looking for, by his sensations at the site) or the Auschwitz concentration camp are good examples for experiencing astral pain/negativity. Certain churches or holy places (e.g., Stonehenge, England; Fatima, Portugal; Zeitoun, Egypt) are examples for the more positive, environmental astral aura/field influences. Every place, outdoors or indoors, that was at any time the site for some intense emotional release (e.g., where somebody was raped) will retain this energy for some time, which can be felt by visitors to the site or even be revived and nourished (e.g., by sensation seekers, a camera crew, and TV viewers all over the country who then look at the newscast, while feeling their own emotional reactions to the event).

Some of us may have experienced the pain and sadness in the church alcove designated for lighting candles for the dead or loved ones in pain. Whether we are mourning or not, it is difficult to not get sad and heavy-hearted if we sit there for a while. This means that many people actually shed and leave behind some of their grief—good for them! In other words, the astral energy field of an area is *fed* energetically by human emotion taken to it. It is maintained and literally *nourished*—good or bad—by the human energy it takes to produce the feelings of grief, anger, pain, joy, reverence, etc. These feelings then have a virtually independent life, if you will; that is, so long as their particular energy quality is replenished by people.

To *dispel* such fields, it is necessary to endow the place with sufficient counter-directed energy, i.e., LOVE, hope, optimism, joy...to counteract depressing or frightening fields (of course, it is not necessary or desirable to dispel healthy and pleasant energy fields). For strong fields nourished by many people over long periods of time, sufficient counter-directed energy might have to be supplied in a concentrated, very specific manner (an exorcism, of sorts), probably repeatedly. Therefore, if we really want to forgive and put behind us the Holocaust of the Third Reich, it would be a good idea to not go to related places to remember, re-experience and *revive the horrors* but, rather, to *heal the places* with counter-directed feeling quality and with it, oneself.

Emotional self-healing comes from the fact that we experience the very energy quality in our own system, as we produce it to heal something or someone else. This is why energy-healing activity, for example, is experienced as highly rewarding by the practitioner—as *all* healing should if done right—or why the surest way to experience love and forgiveness is...*to give it*!

3. The Mental Body

Most of what has been said about the astral body is also true for the mental plane or energy field, *except* that here we deal with *thoughts,* conscious or unconscious. As you might imagine, thoughts are somewhat less colorful, "dryer" than emotions, stripped of much sensational quality, if you will. The mental body is increasingly paler or pastel-colored in or around a healthy, well-developed person. Mental energy is less dense than astral or physical energy, and the energy frequency (vibratory rate) is substantially higher. The mental body, too, is egg-shaped, but extends *beyond* the astral body.

All thoughts are goal-directed or purposive: They always bear the mark (return address) of their maker, as well as an addressee. They are packaged and sent into the environment, to a specific recipient or anywhere within our own organism, as specifically or vaguely as we afford energy (concentration) to do so. The energy that propels thoughts is the *motivation* with which we produce them. Thoughts—more so than feelings—can be seen as highly specific shapes (Leadbeater, C.W. & Besant, A., 1933), e.g., during meditations, when we are sufficiently still and receptive.

> One example from my own experience was a joint regular meditation I did with one of my sisters for a while, at agreed-upon, 30-minute time frames, before leaving Germany. She was so distraught over my impending departure, so that we wanted to rehearse *being together in our minds,* while we were still in the same country. Still, we were many miles apart

> from each other, even while both living in Germany. After each joint meditation, we would call each other up and discuss the experience. For our very first mental get-together, I lay myself down on my back and focused on my *desire* (astral energy) to be with her. Simultaneously, I *visualized* her face and general looks (mental energy). After a while, I had the sensation of my body being pulled and stretched in all kinds of directions, e.g., right arm up, the sense of being diagonally stretched; then the other side...was she *dancing* with me, I wondered? These sensations were quite strong and *independent* of the positioning of my *physical* arms/legs on my bed at the time. Suddenly, all got "quiet" somehow. Then there was a flood of "objects" (black and white, translucent) flying at me, it seemed. They came straight at me, toward (and into?) my face and above-the waist area. This continued for a while and then suddenly stopped.
>
> I was impressed by the experience and quite curious about it. So I called her. She told me that, for the first 15 minutes or so she was standing on her balcony to do some Yoga exercises (the stretching sensations). Since Yoga movements require complete concentration and are quite graceful I perceived them as a *dance*. Then she picked up a book and read me one of her favorite poems (with me as the specific recipient in mind). As a poet puts significant mental energy into the verbal/thought packaging of every idea to be expressed—much more so than we use in everyday conversation—I could see these highly defined, magnificent shapes, literally colorless (pure), none of which were disturbing in any way, and all directed at the higher energy centers (above the waist; more about energy centers or Chakras, as these are called, later). As my sister then read the poem to me again over the phone, it was very evident that it simply *was* a very *beautiful* poem, packaging nothing but the most harmonious and spiritual content into mental expressions.

Of course, the opposite can also be the case, i.e., negative thoughts which are those that confuse (because *they* are confused), or which instill or contain doubt...any "crazy-making" thought content, whether deliberate or unintended by the sender. A bio-energy system has an inherent drive for *one*-ness, wholeness and unity. Therefore, it perceives any doubt, lack of clarity and truth as incongruent and disturbing (note that the term *doubt* is an expression of something *two*-fold). When exposed to negative thought content—either one's own or in the environment—for extended periods, this produces a sense of grinding teeth, like screeching chalk on a blackboard, or like any repeatedly over-extended nerve aches, as only a nerve can ache. If we fail to remove ourselves from the source of such aggravation—including the practice of thought-stopping to discipline our own thinking—negative emotions of anger/frustration or despair/depression are sure to follow. This process carries the disturbance into the astral body and, if not stopped or corrected, it will eventually constrict energy somewhere in the ether and, finally, in the physical body.

What we think and believe over any length of time *is* or *becomes* reality, because it is repeatedly endowed with sufficient energy to create semi-permanent *shapes*. These shapes can be perceived (visually, audibly or intuitively known) when tuning our attention in to someone's mental body. Just as we can become emotionally *drained* in the presence of certain people or places, the same is true for intruding negative thoughts: If we notice that we tend to have ruminating thoughts, every time we are near certain people or places, we should consider the possibility that these thoughts are *not our own,* i.e., that they come from the environment. If these thoughts are disturbing, the worst thing we can do is to take them home with us and to continue brooding about them because, in this fashion, we take them on and *increase* them by endowing them with our own mental energy. *This is how goodness and spiritual wealth, but also how negativity is being spread!*

Thinking *is* doing and hence *observable* on the mental plane. Let me describe a related, personal experience:

> I was doing the dishes at my kitchen sink one evening, as I was entertaining dinner guests. We were all in a very good mood. My ex-husband and some of the guests were standing behind me with kitchen towels in their hands, eager to help, while laughing and kidding around. For a moment—as I was trying to focus on what I was doing, plus thinking about serving dessert afterwards—I must have removed myself mentally from the actual kitchen scene and saw, in an instant, how my ex-husband, in jest, picked up a wrought iron frying pan and swung it in the direction of my behind. The way I saw it, he swung it so hard that it would surely have broken my back, had he actually done it in the physical reality. I stopped breathing for a moment; all in me was incredibly still (incidentally, this is a typical impression when tuning in to one of the other realities, i.e., the sense that time and sometimes

> sound stand still/stop). Then I turned around to face my husband and told him what I had just seen him do. To my surprise (and his), he blushed from ear to ear and then stuttered his admission: The thought of slapping my behind with the pan, which was actually in his hand, had really crossed his mind! Apparently, in the last minute, he decided against it, assuming I would probably not think it funny while I was working so hard.

The mental realm is the energy field where *voices* can be *heard,* where complete messages can be received and where so-called *channeling* originates. The fact that every thought and feeling are observable/audible realities on other realms, is referred to in the Bible: "For nothing is secret, that shall not be made manifest; neither *any thing* hid, that shall not be known and come abroad" (Luke 8:17); and, "Therefore whatsoever ye have spoken in darkness shall be heard in the light; and that which ye have spoken in the ear in closets shall be proclaimed upon the housetops" (Luke 12:3).

Correction and healing of the mental body can be achieved by many of the same methods as work for astral healing: Flower essences and crystals contain a healthy thought component, i.e., *information, essence, melody* or *wisdom* of the plant or crystal, plus there are color and energy therapies. Also, this is where psychotherapy and counseling can do a lot of good by making unconscious thought processes conscious and rehearsing the discipline of the same so that those may change, lastingly. Regular meditation is most useful here, to quiet and soothe current thinking and, instead, to sensitize the person to *alternative thoughts* and ideas. Meditation can *open the door* to completely new attitudes (the combination of thought content with a corresponding feeling quality; i.e., a mental-astral complex or syndrome), previously blocked by compulsive, erroneous thinking. All erroneous thinking is disharmonious; these are thoughts that separate us from our creator: They are about being disconnected from oneself and one's environment, the universe and life itself.

4. The Causal Body

The Causal Body is what some call the *Higher Self.* As the Ether Body acts as a blueprint for the physical body, so does the Causal Body for the human psyche, soul, personality or MIND. The latter terms all mean the same; please refer to the chapter on *Consciousness and the Mind.*

The causal plane of existence facilitates the emergence of pure spirit (original life energy/consciousness) into any kind of *form* or *shape.*

It constitutes the Big Bang, if you will, or the "hole in the Swiss cheese," around which substance (density) forms. Therefore, you may regard the causal plane as a *point,* a *line* or a *field* of very subtle energy, dense enough to no longer be "in heaven," yet—for our coarse understanding—hardly there at all. It is invisible except for the fewest clairvoyants. Beyond the causal plane are the so-called "heavenly spheres" or "heavens," where shape or form serve but *symbolic* representations of cosmic *principles* or *laws*.

When depicted three-dimensionally, the Causal Body around a human being looks as shown in Figure 2: It is very subtle and large, encompassing all other energy bodies. The size depends on a person's degree of physical, mental and spiritual development and well-being. Further, it is *glassy* or *translucent,* containing very pale-pastel but *shiny* colors (Leadbeater, C.W., 1925). With a person's increasing harmony and consciousness, the amount of light, the degree of organization (of colors into beautiful patterns) and the size of the Causal Body increase.

When we try to depict the *causal plane of existence* in relation to the other energy realms in creation, in a two-dimensional fashion, it might look something like in Figures 3a or 3b. However, since the causal plane (or any reality or truth) is *not merely two- or even three-dimensional,* any possible depiction merely represents *degrees of approximation to the truth.* Any and all descriptions we provide in the physical reality will always be lacking something. For example, Figure 3a shows nicely that God (by whatever name) resides *beyond* His creation and that everything develops or unfolds from *Oneness* into *Multiplicity* or *Plurality.* The further the energy or creation is away from God—the source for heat, light and life—the *colder* the energy becomes and the more densely it is compressed. At the same time, the energy frequency or vibratory rate slows down.

Figure 3b is unsuited to reflect all this. Its strength, instead, is that it portrays the idea of a Big Bang: Viewing the causal field as a *point* conveys the idea of a point of emergence, as well as a mirroring effect around it: Everything below this pivotal point is an analogy of sorts of what can be found above it, according to the notion that nothing can exist on earth for which the corresponding *idea* or *principle* does not exist in heaven. This concept is also contained in the Jewish Menorah (in a horizontal fashion): The seven candles representing the seven planes of existence, whereby the center one acts as a pivotal point.

Each Figure is true; yet each contains elements the other one does not capture.

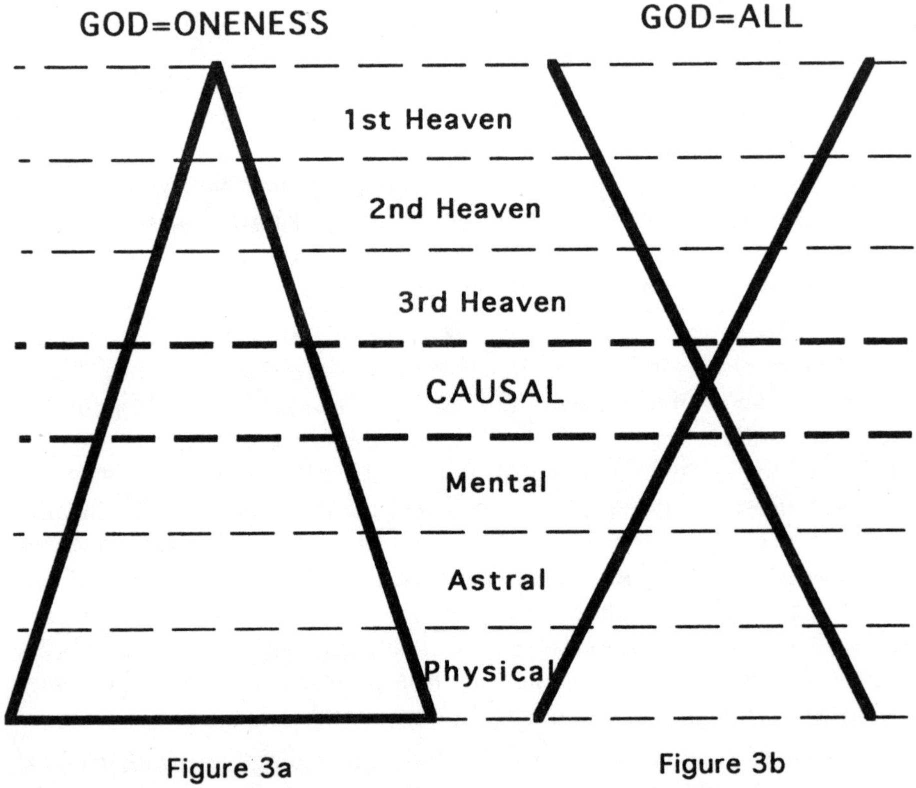

Figure 3: The Seven Planes of Existence

Returning to the Causal Body, let us say that it contains all ideas and intentions *in principle*, in their most abstract form, that a person wishes to manifest or bring into physical shape, form or expression. Ideally and originally, the Causal Body is perfect and whole. However, since all energy bodies are in constant communication with each other (refer to the chapter on *The Chakra System*), in every direction, back *and* forth, persistent negativity on any level below the causal will eventually effect a change in the causal building blocks or intentions. Subsequently, we think, feel and act *as if* we had changed our Mind about our original intentions for being here! Of course, our inherent spirit did not change its "mind" (will) at all, which is why getting in touch with the spirit spark will bring healing (refer to the chapter on *The Spirit Spark*).

> This might be compared to an architect who builds his/her own house and then lives in it a while. S/he might develop desires and ideas for activities and conveniences previously unconsidered and, subsequently, decide to return to the drawing board. S/he pulls out the old plans. By changing something here and there, we might be able to add an exercise room; however, by so doing, we might upset the overall calculations for a carrying wall and plumbing, for example.

If such a change is vastly incongruent with divine harmony and will, disorder will be fed back to the denser energy bodies. The disorder becomes ingrained or permanent, that is until it is counter-acted or corrected somehow.

Correction on the causal level can come in only two ways: One way is that we try to change something *most persistently*, in the *here and now* (i.e., in the physical reality), in an apparent problem area. This usually involves a tremendous show of willpower, coupled with insight and at least *some* spiritual guidance and intervention, e.g., prayer and honest self-assessment, which can be aided by an intact support system of honest, loving relatives and friends. Also, to effect the desired change, this process might involve an entire lifetime.

The best example for this is probably *alcoholism* or any drug addiction. Healing involves:

- *Physically*, abstaining from the drug. Interrupting actual, physical behaviors, like pouring the drink and/or administering the drug.
- On the *astral and mental levels*, emotional and mental changes (i.e., *attitude* changes) concerning drug use, people (e.g., fear of them) and life in general.

- On the *causal plane,* healing *must* include such abstract concepts as humility, honesty, goodwill, acceptance, tolerance which are quite *spiritual in nature*! Prayer and meditation (addressed to *some* power greater than ourselves) are the main facilitators of this goal.

Only when attending to a problem on *all* levels/realms of existence, i.e., all components of the disorder, can healing have any permanence and be the best it can be for that person. This is how and why 12-step programs have a greater potential to work than any other commonly used treatment for drug addiction alone. However, this principle is true for any and all disorders. At this point, we can only guess the extent to which the number of relapses and healing time in general might be reduced for *any* illness; surgery, medications and recurrence of illness *elsewhere* in the body might be avoided; and patients might be made more comfortable while recovering, if we only attended to *all* facets of their particular disorder/disharmony.

The only other way to effect change in the Causal Body is to find a healer who is capable to *reach* and influence very directly the causative energy factor contained on this realm. Of course, this can only be done by means of bio-energy work and must *still* be coupled—usually—with the appropriate attitude and behavior changes to not immediately undo the energy work again. However, the attitude and behavior changes come much more easily *with* the help of such energy work. In fact, for persons who are only marginally cognitive or not cognitive at all (e.g., comatose patients), this may be the *only* treatment possible.

Reiki, Chakra Therapy, Energy-Balancing/Harmonizing, Therapeutic Touch and even Regression/ Reincarnation Therapies are all *energy therapies*. However, not every energy therapist automatically treats all energy bodies. Which one(s) s/he affects has a lot to do with *who* the therapist *is,* as a person and spirit entity. Each healer has unique specialties and talents, but also limitations. Therefore, some shopping around may be necessary. Considering the level of specialization in all areas of the helping professions, this should not come as a surprise: We also would not take our breast tumor to a dentist or use a Freudian analyst as our sole treatment to combat alcoholism, would we?

A summary of the human energy fields/bodies and some of their characteristics is attempted in Table 1. Furthermore:

- Each field or plane is subdivided into 7 sub-planes, which are probably again subdivided by 7, infinitely. For healing purposes, however, this has been of little significance, except for knowing that, in the physical realm,

<table>
<tr><th>Plane</th><th>Mode</th><th>Color</th><th>Density</th><th>Size</th></tr>
<tr><td>CAUSAL</td><td>Prompting/Intent:
Principle (Essence)
“Abstract”</td><td>Pale, Pastel
White</td><td rowspan="6">Low
I
N
C
R
E
A
S
E
High</td><td rowspan="6">Large
D
E
C
R
E
A
S
E
Small</td></tr>
<tr><td></td><td></td><td></td></tr>
<tr><td>MENTAL</td><td>Thinking/Motivation:
Goals/Purpose
“Logical”</td><td>Pastel</td></tr>
<tr><td>ASTRAL</td><td>Feeling/Motivation:
Emotions
“Exciting”</td><td>Iridescent,
Bright</td></tr>
<tr><td></td><td></td><td></td></tr>
<tr><td>ETHER/
PHYSICAL</td><td>Physical
“Double”
Manifestation:
Expression/Form
“Doing”</td><td>Shiny,
Silver/Gray</td></tr>
</table>

Table 1: Summary of Energy Body Characteristics

we distinguish between the sub-planes of *mineral, plant, animal and human life, plus three etheric fields of decreasing density.*

- These fields should not be viewed as being layered on top of each other. Rather, they *permeate each other.* A more subtle field always *permeates and extends beyond* the denser one(s).
- These bodies are part of the human reality, *at least as much* as the physical reality, *if not more so.* We exist on these other realms *all the time,* even though we usually are not aware of them except in dreams. In truth, however, these bodies are much more *real* than our physical one, in that *they are eternal* (all but the ether body)! As such, they contain the memory of any physical incarnation on earth or experience ever, anywhere in the cosmos. We have *simultaneous lives* or consciousnesses, so to speak. For our other (not focused on the physical reality) consciousnesses, our present physical "reality" is the dream! For everything we do, think and feel in the physical reality, there are corresponding acts, happenings and consequences on all other realms. The same is true the other way around, i.e., what we do during and with our physical life and body is as much a *consequence* of as it is *causing* who we are in our non-physical realities.
- Our subtle energy bodies obey non-physical laws; i.e., in and with them, we have capabilities *above and beyond the space and time concepts* as we know them. Feelings are overt, visible realities, and thinking is doing: Thinking of a person is to be instantly with that person, regardless of distance or walls that may physically separate us, with the particular thoughts *and* emotions we may have about them. For us who are physically incarnated beings, certain etheric components may also "travel" along, e.g., the scent of the perfume we wear at the time or tobacco smoke. We *all* react to such subtle energy presence, whether we are consciously aware of it or not. Without knowing why, we might get nervous, angry or uncomfortable if the presence is negative or unpleasant. Contrarily, we might suddenly calm down and develop optimism in the midst of a most difficult situation, if the presence is well-meaning, loving and supportive. The more sensitive among us can actually identify the presence, especially one they already know well. In any event, these added capabilities in non-physical realms explain all so-called extra-sensory experiences, e.g., knowing who the caller is as the telephone rings, or perceiving a person's glance at us from behind, even at great distance.
- It is due to the fewer limitations in those non-physical realms/bodies, that *healing at a distance* (so-called remote, distant or non-local therapies) is possible. Healers who deliberately utilize their knowledge of their subtle

energy capabilities, can "read" and treat clients from wherever they physically happen to be. This is also how prayer works, as well as—unfortunately—energy sent for less benign purposes, e.g., specific curses and general ill-will. Thoughts and emotions are always intricately connected with their sender as well as with their designated recipient, unless that "addressee" rigorously refuses (with his/her entire being) to accept these. Benevolent thoughts/emotions sent to people who are temporarily too constricted to accept and utilize these, can resort to them at a later time, during a moment of "surrender" and "enlightenment." A prayer or healing energy remains as a positive resource around the addressee, unless deliberately rejected to the sender. Unfortunately, the same is true for negativity which remains around the addressee as a source of misfortune, aggravation and ill health.

- The *motivation* and *reasons behind* our deeds and creations, including our thoughts and feelings, are the essence of our true being. They give everything we do and are a "flavor" and a direction. This facilitates the learning *content* which is the only thing that "we can take with us" and hence really exists. For example, the energy alone it takes to be curious about something—curiosity being the desire or expectation to know something, long before we formulate a specific question—propels thoughts and feelings into a particular direction. Curiosity is a *feeling quality*, the energy of which carries our questions, once formulated, to the very realm where they have a chance to be answered: "Ask, and it shall be given you; seek, and ye shall find; knock, and it shall be opened unto you" (Luke 11:9). This is how we "attract" and invite situations, people and things into our lives—actually *we* go to *them*! This is how the light bulb was invented or how Einstein "discovered" his Theory of Relativity. Although not many of our creations and inventions are awarded much worldly attention, we do *create constantly*, by means of our physical, astral and mental energies, which is how we define ourselves to the world and universe around us. This is how we give ourselves shape or form energetically. Our creations (or the lack of the same, for our omission to decide or act at times) reflect back to us our conscious motives and reasons, as well as the unconscious ones which will manifest themselves as "unwanted side effects." Thus we have an opportunity to "look into the mirror" and to "recognize ourselves in our creations," i.e., to learn more about ourselves by making the unconscious conscious. Unfortunately, in the face of unwanted side-effects, we are often inclined to disassociate ourselves from our product and blame/project the causative motivations on to others.

- *No thought or emotion is in vain,* as is no energy ever, no matter what we spend it on. It all has effects beyond our wildest dreams and it pays well to become more aware of just what it is we do or fail to do on other realms of our existence. Last but not least, thus is the purpose of life: Learning to become completely aware.

B. THE SPIRIT SPARK

Not too much will be said here about the spirit spark—a minuscule amount of the purest, divine energy/information located in the human heart, as it does not require *healing* or contribute to *dis*-orders. It originates from and is forever connected with the heavenly spheres and is our *Guiding Light* or the *God within* any one of us. However, it should be noted that it is unique to human beings; animals do not possess it.

This spark can, to date, not be measured or made visible; it can, however, be felt on occasions, e.g., when we desperately seek it or when God wants to shake us up a bit. The latter can come at a moment when we are just about to commit a significant error, e.g., as a reminder or warning. It is completely painless and feels like a pounding or punch in the middle of the chest.

> In 1987, at a very low point in my life, I entered into individual psychotherapy. What I did not know at the time was that I had chosen an energy worker and very spiritual person as my facilitator. However, as the saying goes, *there are no coincidences* in God's universe, including on earth!
>
> I was a very depressed and frightened person. One day, after an energy session, we were talking about the concept of *ego* and of overcoming it by letting something else reign my life instead. Tears welled up in my eyes as I mumbled that, if it were not for my ego, there would be no reason for me to get up in the morning any more. "What else *is* there?" I asked, completely distraught. At that moment, still comfortably stretched out and completely relaxed on the massage table, something swelled in my chest. As it quickly rose up into my throat, it choked me a bit. Simultaneously, I "saw" a golden "blob" right beneath my face, inside of me. Luckily, my therapist had just turned away and was not looking at me, for I had absolutely no control over my face or anything that I had known as "me" while this was happening. As it swelled and stretched to make itself known to me, it reminded me of an

amoeba as I had once seen it in a biology book. From that day on, I *knew* my spirit spark, that and how it wants to love and guide me from within, and I fondly named it, "my amoeba."

C. CONSCIOUSNESS AND THE MIND

One of the most common errors of today is to associate the "mind" too closely with the human brain, perhaps to even equate the two, i.e., to assume the "I" or the sense of self is *in* the physical brain. However, we are not our brains. "I" is not a strange, gray mass of flesh located in my skull, unless I absolutely *want* this to be so. Remember: Thinking is doing and thus becomes our reality. Think of yourself as a 3-dimensional brain, and your consciousness will be accordingly limited. In truth, we can think and feel ourselves into most anything we choose, but it would be a mistake to completely identify with that object, being, organ or tissue. We are mentally and emotionally capable to "step into the shoes" of some other organism or object due to the inter-connectivity of all things, due to the fact that all comes, ultimately, from one and the same source. However, when we have completed the exercise and satisfied our curiosity, we will again slip into our individual separateness, i.e., will perceive also those things that make us different from each other, in addition to those things we apparently share and can identify with. I can think myself into my brain or liver (can step into its "shoes," experience its functioning/purpose), but this is merely a mental and emotional exercise. In the end, there is my brain and my liver, separate from me, and "I" remain "I" during and after a liver transplant, brain damage and most certainly when my body dies.

A second error is to equate the mind with merely our *conscious* awareness of self and the world. Statements like, "It slipped my mind," imply that the mind is viewed as some conscious entity from which information can slip into some unconscious realm or never-never land. Just *where* does something go that slips the mind? What happens to it? Is it still part of me and my mind, or who owns it while I cannot think of it? If it leaves me and my mind altogether, how can it be that we are able to retrieve it again, at some later time (usually when we least expect it, i.e., after we abandoned our *conscious* search for the information)? A shortcoming of all schools of personality, ego, self and mind is that none truly *localizes* any of these abstract concepts *in relation to our physical bodies*. No wonder we have never been able to even begin *measuring* it. To make the mind tangible and "real," it requires an operational definition. I am suggesting, therefore, that:

> "I" am my total Mind (with a capital M), the total awareness possible while being physically incarnated. This Mind is comprised of my total conscious and unconscious, hence *the sum of my subtle energy bodies.*

This total Mind, then, lends itself to be measured and expressed in terms of energy frequencies or vibratory rate, in whatever units that can be assigned to these. The same frequencies can manifest themselves as sound, color, smell and tactile sensations, thoughts and feelings, depending on the sensitivity and "expertise" of a medium (a radio or a camera, an eye or an ear, a brain or a heart). This is to say that we can observe and correlate a variety of observations to abstract from them certain regularities: For example, we might validate that the color pink—as clairvoyantly observed around people—matches their self-statements of experiencing loving feelings/thoughts, as well as determining the particular energy frequency, intensity and location in/around the body. This will make thoughts, feelings and a variety of sensations measurable/tangible—if not love itself—in ways heretofore considered impossible. In the past, clairvoyant observations have been correlated with medical diagnoses (Karagulla, S. and van Gelder Kunz, D., 1989); I suggest we broaden the *spectrum of measurability.*

Conscious awareness, then, is what people commonly refer to as the mind. It can be visualized as an area involving the physical brain, plus a segment of all subtle energy bodies, as shown in Figure 4. In truth, this "wedge" is not so neat. Rather, it contains elements or individual points from everywhere in our subtle energy fields. These points are selected and connected to each other in a fashion that makes sense to each of us, individually. They exclude contradicting information to a large degree. We attempt to consolidate, understand or hold these points together via the human brain and readily accessible, rational thinking processes, coupled with memory storage and retrieval mechanisms. Unfortunately, it is nearly impossible to visually demonstrate such a multi-dimensional construct.

Similarly, yet more arbitrarily selected, are the points of information tidbits that comprise the human ego. It is more arbitrary in that it may include elements from *outside* one's own energy bodies, e.g., when we attempt to imitate someone else or truly confuse ourselves with others through over-identification with them. The ego is also more *stubborn* than the common "I" awareness/mind in that it is usually *older* than conscious, rational thinking (according to psychologists, ego development takes place during our earliest childhood years) and not always conscious. Because much of it is *unconscious,* it is not nearly as logical (hence appears more

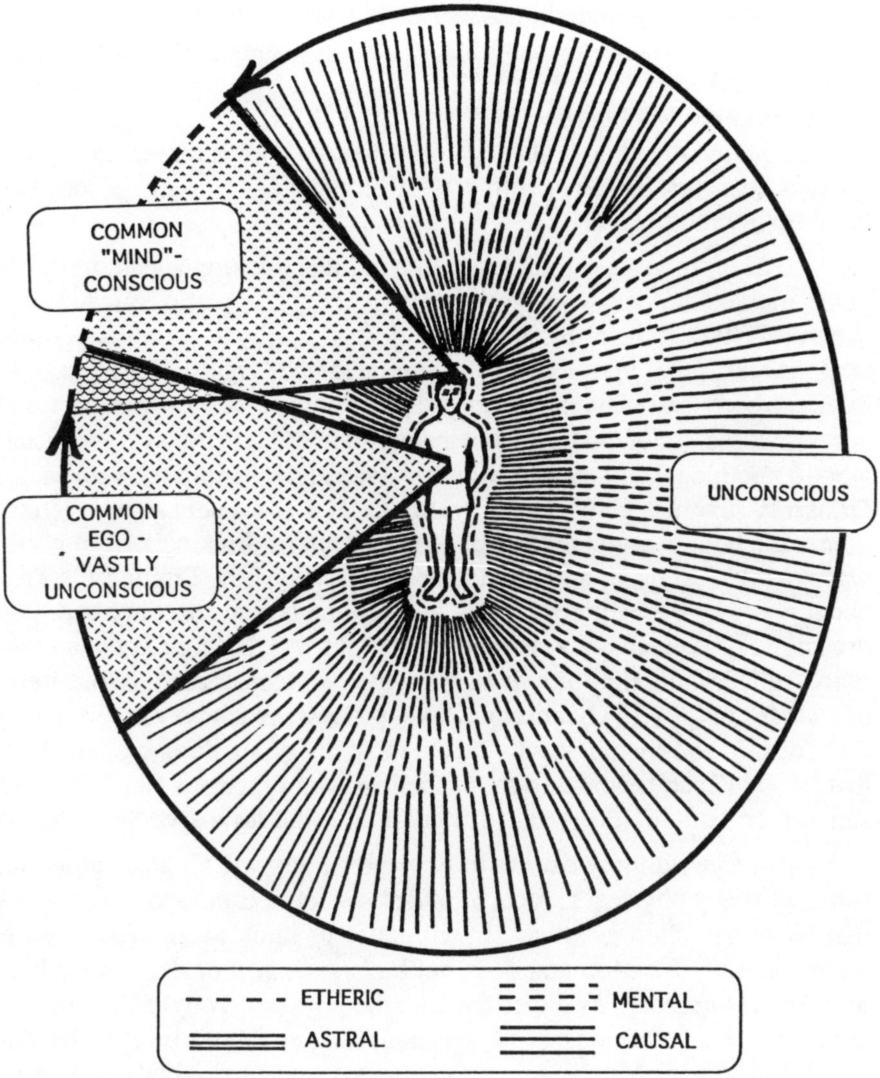

Figure 4: Conscious/Unconscious Mind and the Ego

arbitrary) than the conscious awareness. The ego is a necessary, although imaginary and gut-driven construct, while we have no idea who we are and what we are about as individuals and social/spiritual beings, unaware of our unique and our shared characteristics. It is an assumed "I" which we subsequently test via trial and error: E.g., if I assume (for not really knowing) that I resemble Michael Jackson and, if I like everything he stands for, I shall subsequently change this ego only when I realize that certain characteristics (e.g. my hairdo) conflict with other things I want—a job, being liked by my mother, etc.

The ego can access our brain (the rational thinking apparatus or computer, incl. data/memory banks) as well as any other part of our Mind can. When it is the ego resorting to the brain, it is usually to formulate rationalizations and "good reasons" for its continued and "rightful" existence. Our physical body can make itself known to our conscious awareness, too, by accessing the brain and stimulating certain thought processes—usually when something is unbalanced which we can alleviate through some action: Drinking, running, going to the restroom. If I am a person who tends to ignore the body's needs for fluids, I may dream of drinking a huge glass of water while feeling how tremendously satisfying it is. Similarly, a dream about going to the bathroom might awaken me before I wet my bed. Fever dreams very typically reveal the actual fight that goes on between white blood cells and foreign intruders, allowing us a conscious glimpse into an otherwise completely unconscious body process. When we are seriously ill, the illness is and should usually be the most important thing on our Mind at that time; "I" can become aware of the involved processes and consciously support the body in its efforts with my total Mind for a speedier recovery.

We can willingly *choose* to *think* about any and all areas of the total Mind, plus any physical aspects of ourselves. Yet it is not the physical brain that picks and chooses what "it" will store or think about. The brain has mere computer function and does not have such will or deliberate choice. Instead, it is *operated by* either the ego, the physical (body) sub-consciousness, any part (conscious or unconscious) of our Mind, or even by other people's minds or Minds. Any component of our total Mind can theoretically access this computer, *unless* our common mind (conscious awareness only) interferes by means of its free choice and will. Yet even then, the unconscious mind will forever try to gain access to conscious awareness, especially if it is of vital importance for one's safety, health or emotional happiness, e.g., by means of dreams (while the common mind is vastly incapacitated) or by creating all kinds of accidents and other circumstances aimed at getting our conscious attention, *in order to prevent worse circum-*

stances and/or to stimulate spiritual growth. Common "re-Minders" (messages from the Mind) are: "Freudian slips" of the tongue or more tragic accidents and, of course, physical illness, aches and pains. Tuning our conscious mind into our unconscious areas will open all our senses to others' unconscious areas. We begin to sense people's motives and underlying patterns, pleasant or unpleasant, as soon as we have acquainted ourselves consciously with our own, related motives and patterns. As we become aware of and clean our own house, spirit material and activity in *all* things becomes increasingly noticeable. Training our finer, intuitive faculties inevitably makes us "psychic." Unfortunately, this is today considered an *abnormality,* rather than a normal, necessary and therefore desirable by-product of human development and redemption itself. We are to become the clean vessels through which God's spirit can shine—what else can this possibly mean but that we are all to become—at some point—walking mediums, channeling all the time, as Christ modeled for us, each according to our own thumb-print/specialty: Singing, dancing, painting, the gift of gab, healing, teaching, serving and sharing in every profession/occupation...and a compassionate way of living and treating each other in general. To manifest beauty and goodness on earth, I must have keen senses to assess the same, as well as the ability to recognize and ward off distractions, on all planes of existence. Developing my "psychic" abilities, then, is nothing more than the necessary tools (muscles) I receive along the way, if I keep moving and do not stunt my development. They are our birthright—*gifts* waiting to be claimed, as we are learning to consciously "move into" our spirit bodies. They can not, however, be claimed through any shortcuts: Temporarily and prematurely removing our *blinders* (e.g., through the use of mind-altering drugs or a variety of metaphysical experiments) can be coupled with a high price tag, as we neither know what we are perceiving nor what to do with it. The result can be disastrous, leaving us confused and more vulnerable than before, if not insane.

The Mind—the sum total of our astral, mental and causal energy bodies—is synonymous with the so-called Soul: IT IS WHO I REALLY AM, ALWAYS WAS AND WILL BE. The Mind or Soul has existed prior to our physical birth(s) and is the entity that lives on. A great many mystics have pondered throughout the ages, "Does the body have a soul, or does the soul have a physical body? Is the soul in the body, or is the body in the soul"? The answer is, "Both." The body is in the soul. However, as all subtle energies permeate the denser ones, they also permeate the physical body. The soul/Mind is within and without the physical body. No physical body can live without a soul; however the soul lives very well without a physical body.

The Mind does not require a physical brain in order to "think" or be aware of itself. Contrarily, when the physical thinking machine goes to sleep (or dies), awareness is greatly enhanced, if not immediately total. Without actually dying, we can evidence this nightly in dreams, out-of-body experiences (e.g., travel through the planes of existence), etc. With or without concurrent, measurable brain waves, we think and are constantly aware of ourselves, of feeling, being and living; we make decisions, we remember, we interact... . It is a complete myth that we dream only during REM phases (with concurrent rapid eye movements and measurable brain wave activity): WE ARE, FEEL, THINK AND DO, ON ALL PLANES OF EXISTENCE, while asleep or awake, whether physically alive or dead. In summary, we exist much more "there" than "here," qualitatively and quantitatively. We need only tune our conscious mind in to these realities/energy frequencies.

> By tuning our "denser" components in to the subtleties of existence, one step at a time, these denser components themselves become elevated, purified, finer, enhanced and less limited than they were before. They "catch on," which is the very mechanism and purpose of redemption and transcendence: By the time we discard this physical body, all our components, including the flesh, are to be elevated one notch in terms of energy frequency, from where each started out in this physical life.

For this spiritual development to take place, everything we do, think, feel and subject ourselves to (incl. food and the environment) is extremely important, as well as *how* we do it and *with whom* we do it: We are to pick and choose those things for ourselves that are helping to facilitate this goal, rather than deterring from it. We are to constantly ask and answer these questions for ourselves: "Is what I am confronted with light and uplifting, or does it add weight to my life? Does it drag me down and 'retard' me, or is it inspiring and stimulating?"

The greatest deterrent from spiritual development is *fear,* fear being the result of blind spots in our Mind. They remain blind spots so long as I am afraid of them. We might fear what (horrible) things we may find if we only looked. We might fear to lose control for not being able to sort out the conflict resulting from discoveries which may potentially contradict our conscious, common mind. We fear change. We fear to be traumatized by "monsters."

I had heard so much about elves and fairies but could not remember ever having consciously seen one. One day, sitting in my garden, I was praying: "Didn't you promise me, Christ, that you would fulfill any wish, anything at all, if I call upon you? Then please grant me this one and let me see an elf." After a long, profound silence, I felt a voice within, one I had known all my life: "My dear Lilo, know how you always frighten yourself so...(he reminded me of several of my responses to previous encounters with non-physical entities). Know that elves are not alone on that realm. If you see *them*, you will see all else that houses there... ." I immediately understood, shivered for a moment and decided to postpone my wish for a while longer; I was not yet ready. Strangely, however, my left hand which had been resting in the grass, was suddenly very warm and I could distinctly feel several tiny fingers around a finger.

D. THE CHAKRA SYSTEM: COMMUNICATION WITHIN AND BETWEEN MINDS

If thinking and feeling is possible without a physical brain, then it is also true that the Mind can communicate very directly, bypassing the physical brain or mouth, with other Minds, those of planets, animals, plants or persons (incarnated or not)—with EVERYTHING THAT EXISTS. It commands a sophisticated system to make itself aware throughout its subtle energy bodies of varying energy densities, of everything within it. At the same time, it makes itself known to everything around us, indeed, to the entire universe.

1. Communication within one Chakra System

How does information *travel* from one plane of existence to another, from one energy body to the next? How does the energy frequency become *transformed* and communicable from denser to more subtle fields and *vice versa*?

To accomplish these tasks, we are equipped with a most sophisticated system of inter-connecting energy transformers, energy whirlpools, each rotating with a particular speed (sound, light/color), in a particular direction (clockwise and counter-clockwise): The so-called *Chakras*. The term *Chakra* is widely used in the West and easy to pronounce in English. I suggest we adopt it.

The location of our seven main Chakras is shown in Figure 5. Gently

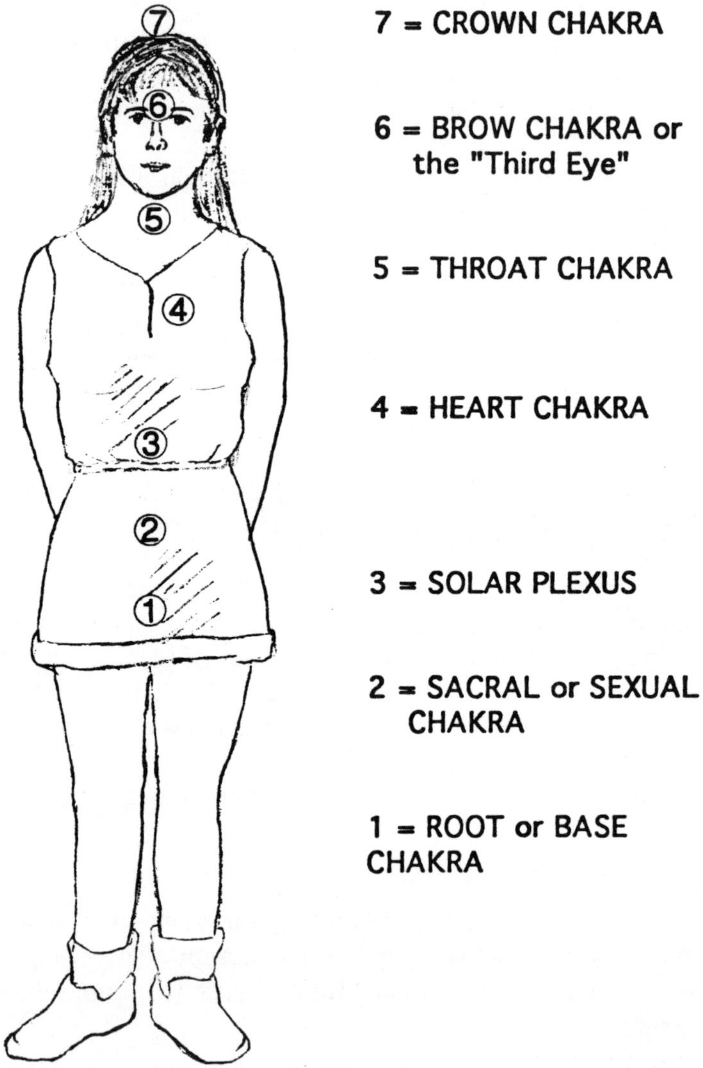

Figure 5: The Seven Main Chakras

sensing with our hands—moving them very slowly a few inches over someone's body—will detect them, i.e., by temperature change (heat, cold) or a light pressure/resistance against the hand. The sensitive healer can further sense the rotation, size and irregularities, e.g., no energy flow/blockages. Some healers use pendulum dowsing to make Chakra activities visible to the physical eye, for a faster assessment.

Each of the main Chakras corresponds to one particular plane of existence or, rather, it is the "antenna" (receiver *and* transmitter) for one of our energy bodies. Therefore, each Chakra specifically vibrates/rotates in the very energy frequency prevalent in the realm for which it is the "expert." From the Base or Root to the Crown, this can be detected as increasing speed of rotation, more scintillating colors, and an increasing number of *facets* (which look like spokes in the wheel of a bicycle; sometimes they are compared with petals in a flower, e.g., the Lotus blossom).

These Chakras link our subtle energy bodies together. All seven are represented in every subtle energy body—all communicate information back and forth—whereby each one is the main communicator for a particular kind of information (or information "density"):

Root/Base	Earth, physical realm/body (incl. ether); rootedness; sense of safety; relationship to/with natural life processes; autonomous bodily processes
Sacral/Astral	Astral plane/body; feelings, emotions, sensations (positive or negative); *Joie de Vivre;* zest; creativity (or depression). Also: Seat of mystical memory, spiritual history and ancestry
Solar Plexus	Mental plane/body; thoughts (usually filtered by the ego first); "opinions"; prejudices/judgments
Heart	Causal plane/body; love; compassion; ability to step into someone else's shoes; intuitive knowing; or lack of any of the above. Also: Potential for accessing universal/divine information *to be* manifested (yet to be given shape/form)
Throat	3rd Heaven; fear/fearlessness of being and expressing myself
Brow/"Third Eye"	2nd Heaven; (in)ability and (un)willingness to see through the eyes of the spirit and to apply its will
Crown	1st Heaven; degree of spirit consciousness

These Chakras act as our *sensory and signaling equipment* (in/out) on subtle energy echelons, for the purpose of assessing truth. As we have the physical five senses to assess our physical reality, the Chakras serve to assess non-physical reality or realities. They can signal by means of sound, color, smell, tactile sensations, symbolic representation (images, shapes, "visions"), and intuitive knowing ("I just *knew* you would say that!"), IN THE ABSENCE OF ANY PHYSICAL STIMULI. Furthermore, we can apparently process them and react to them without involving our conscious awareness, sensory equipment (the physical eyes, ears, etc.) or the brain. A meditating person, tuning in to other realms of existence, might have all kinds of visions or other impressions, without any corresponding (physical) eye movements or brain activity. In fact, we know that the brain must be held *constant* at a particular brain wave state in order to be able to tune our conscious awareness in to our Chakra activity. In dreams as well as meditations and many forms of holistic therapies, we tune the physical brain *out* from, but our conscious awareness *in* to non-physical realities, in order to heal misinformation (disharmony, negativity) contained in them. Learning *is* possible without conscious awareness. However, involving consciousness is more effective and certainly faster.

> When we meditate into our astral, mental or causal bodies, we become aware of the "total picture" around anything we do or *think* we believe. I may think (in my physical, conscious reality) that I absolutely love my job. In a meditative state, "listening" to myself through my Chakras, I may hear different, additional voices which I have previously ignored or deafened with my more domineering voices, "fabricated" opinions and "better" judgments. There may be fears of particular things and people in relation to my job, or talents I am yearning to unfold but cannot in my present circumstances. There may be situations that certain parts of me find completely unbearable at times. I may remember hurtful situations which I had completely "swallowed" and absorbed, without reaction—perhaps someone treated me arrogantly, depriving me of dignity or infringing upon my God-given, free will. When any of these impressions went unnoticed by my conscious awareness and my more "accustomed" mode of assessing my circumstances, they will forever try to "talk" to us afterwards. During meditation and many forms of holistic therapies, this talk is facilitated. Once aware, I can take steps and make changes in my life that do *all of me* justice and account for *all* voices within me.

In the average person living in the north-western, head-oriented hemisphere today, the subtle energy bodies are likely to show energy/vitality irregularities. There is usually significant vitality around the head (if this is where we mentally locate our self), perhaps the hands (true for people who perceive themselves as doers, who associate their hands with power of some kind), the Solar Plexus (seat of the ego) and often around the much suppressed or misguided, but very much alive sexual areas (the lower abdomen). Energy blockages or very little energy are common in the spinal base area (connectivity with the earth and natural life processes), the heart ("use it or lose it") and the throat (due to generalized fear of life/each other). By listening to suppressed voices, we send energy to undernourished areas. This process can be supported my means of many holistic methods that add the missing/healing information to the system. Just as physical food contains energy (= information) which it adds to my total system, so does pharmaceutical medicine, as do self-affirmations, and energy in the environment. We can add information homeopathically, through aromas, by means of a healer's hands and unconditional love, music, etc., etc.

The seven main Chakras are not the only Chakras we have, but they represent the major linkage between energy bodies, with the purpose of communicating. In addition, there are many, many more smaller Chakras, e.g., in every joint, every major organ (e.g., the kidneys), inside the palm of our hands and feet, with mini-Chakras even on every finger tip.

2. Communication with the Environment

In Table 2, I have attempted to illustrate that, on every plane of existence, there is one of the main Chakras opening to the "outside," able to perceive of and deal with information outside our own Mind. Statements like, "It is *only* in your Mind," indicate how little we actually *want* this communication in our society of individualistic striving and separateness, if not to say egocentrism. Indeed, the presence of subtle energy manifestations makes itself known to the Mind, long before they become physically manifest, if they ever do. If they never manifest themselves physically, this does not mean they are not there, that they do not exist! Since all energy is intelligent information, it *wants* to communicate a message or message *impulse*. What of it we are able to perceive depends on us, the fine-tuning of our "receivers" and on our "specialization" (e.g., sound, light, visions, etc.). A telephone, by itself, will not receive radio waves; similarly, a non-musical person may not hear astral music. But then again, he/she may. What is important here is to note that every person decodes, interprets and responds to subtle energies according to their very own personality make-up, degree of consciousness, unique talents and values. If, for example, during the

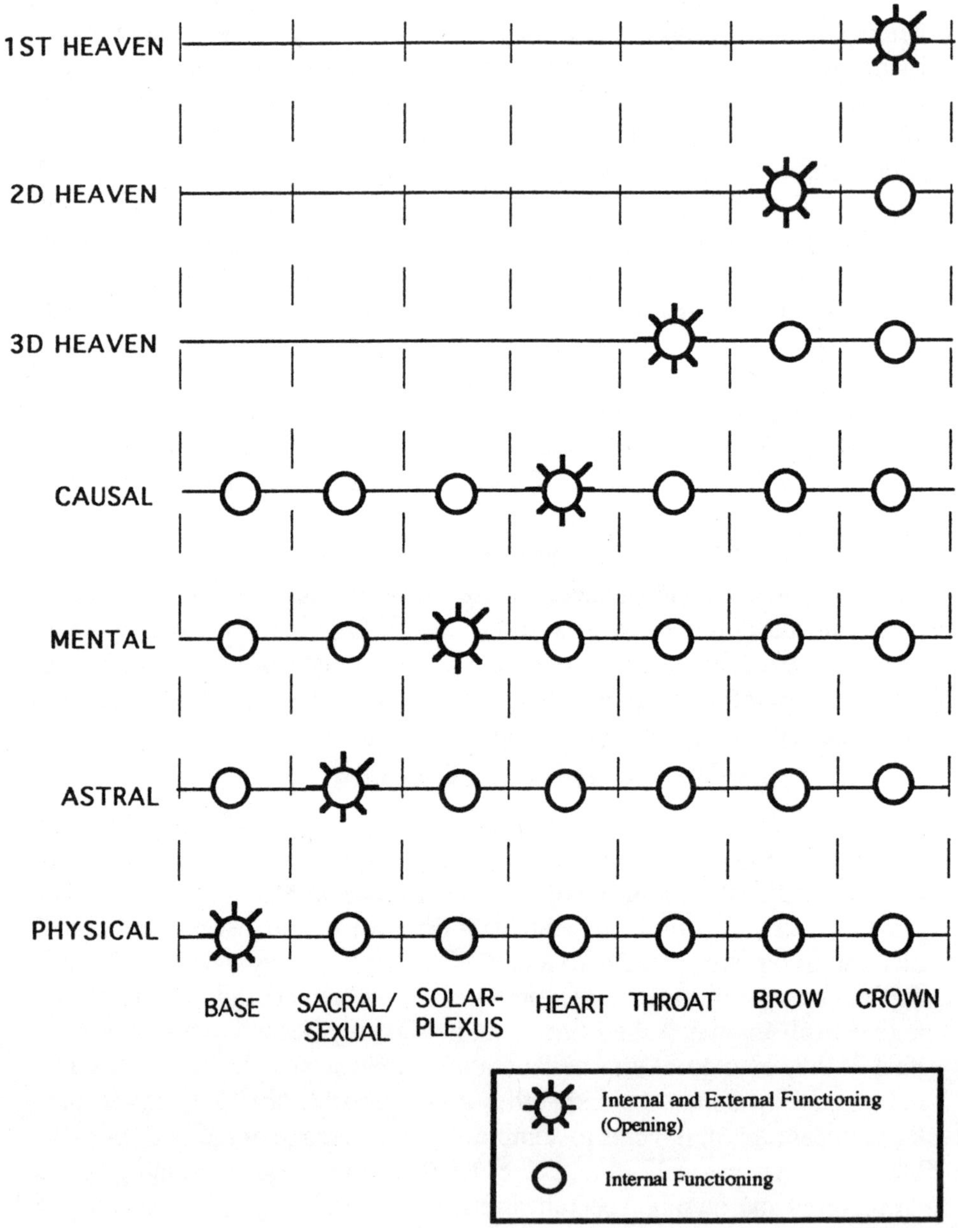

Table 2: Interaction of Main Chakras with the Environment

times of the Old Testament, most people were merely able to perceive of a fearsome God, then this has less to do with God than with the receiver and more to do with the impulses they are able to incorporate into their systems in a fashion that makes sense to them. God, of course, has always been loving and forgiving, in addition to wrathfully protecting love itself. Yet, at the time, most people only recognized power which reigned through intimidation.

By far not all subtle energy impulses we are bombarded with are divine messages, starting with electromagnetic pollution. But then, it is in our self-interest to know and distinguish them from healthy, *helping* impulses. We learn to consciously use the faculties of our subtle energy bodies in much the same manner as we learn to use the physical body, from sitting to walking, from waddling to running and jumping flights of stairs at a time. We learn not to touch an open flame or hot surfaces and to detect rotten food or a chicken bone in our mouth before we swallow it. We learn to distinguish between what helps and what hurts us. So it is in the subtle energy realm. In other words, rather than convincing mental patients in hospitals that their hallucinations are not really real, a more effective treatment would include to take these subtle energy impressions and impulses *more* seriously, so that the patient can finally learn to deal with them. By strengthening our sense of distinction, coupled with the power of free will and choice, the Mind is quite capable *and* responsible to erect boundaries that keep out unwanted, harmful intruders. Besides being immensely beneficial to the patient, this would also be congruent with good, empathic counseling theory, i.e., to accept non-judgmentally the world of another and try to work *with* it.

We are in a dynamic relationship with everything that exists by means of our Chakra system and our Mind, all of the time. If we choose to tune subtle energy impulses out, this doesn't mean they to not intrude us. Quite to the contrary. This, too, represents a relationship—choosing to ignore intrusions is an open invitation! Apart from the poisons we are involuntary bombarded with, we actively attract energy impulses from all realms of existence, as well as other Minds, according to the principle:

LIKE TO LIKE

We learn about our-*Selves* (Minds) from what we consciously attract and inadvertently "let in." We grant entry to information/manipulation because we have "like stuff" contained in our Mind. This *like stuff*, when it is unconscious, usually represents a contradiction to some other stuff we want to manifest consciously. The only way to fix my boundaries, then, is to literally "make up my Mind" about this contradiction. Our Mind continuously takes note of all of these intrusions and contradictions. We can choose to ignore it or we can decide to listen.

We do not have to meditate incessantly to discover our own suppressed voices or messages intruding from the outside. Once we start listening to our inner detection mechanism, the louder and ever-present its signals become. As a result, we will be able to more readily respond to them. What used to take us a week (sometimes years) to discover, digest and finally respond to ("*Why* didn't I say/do...?!"), will become a much faster, more complete evaluation and response. In time, I can do it instantaneously. What prevents us from responding appropriately in any situation is, once again, our blind spots. For example, sometimes crying *is* the most appropriate response. It is completely unnatural (and dishonest) to so desperately *not* reflect back to an aggressor what he/she is doing to us. With it ("Boys don't cry" or "I must avoid the 'emotional woman' label"), I am overriding my perception and the appropriate response, *as well as withholding the honest feedback from each other,* the mirror which allows people to experience their effects on others. How will an inconsiderate person ever learn of their blind spot—inconsideration—when we continually withhold that feedback?

In the above example, I learn about my own rudeness—toward *myself*—by means of a person's rudeness toward me. In this fashion, I inadvertently support that person's rudeness and all rudeness in the world! By reflecting the rudeness back to the sender, I give myself a clearer definition, profile or boundaries than I had before. I become recognizable as I recognize myself. At the same time, I confront my environment with its respective mirrors. A person's negative energy, blocked enough times, will eventually not intrude us any longer. Perhaps, in view of my feedback to them, they might even abandon their negative ways. The faster I stop enabling negative behaviors and attitudes by reflecting them back to the sender, the faster a person can detect and change their injurious ways. At a very minimum, they will have to leave us alone. And, as soon as I detect and fix the hole (blind spot) in my boundaries, they will.

THE SAME PRINCIPLE APPLIES TO ANY AND ALL NEGATIVITY/ DISHARMONY, IN WHATEVER SUBTLE ENERGY FORM IT MAY PESTER US.

While we usually carry out our conflicts with living *persons*—at least we *think* so—in reality, our conflict is mostly about *subtle energies* which that person radiates. Better yet, it is about my apparent inability to detect, distinguish and finally block/reflect back out of my Mind what has inadvertently intruded and is unpalatable. If my Mind cannot *digest* something, it must reject and eliminate it, so that it can continue to function in a healthy way. While we may not be able to stop people from what they do (due to their inherent free will), we close our subtle energy boundaries by assuming a clear position toward the energy impulses which another person sends our way. There are no other boundaries to be had than those of the Mind. Besides erecting *physical* walls (which is highly ineffective as protection against subtle energy), these are the only other boundaries we have and *must* have.

As noted, physical *places* may be infested with negative energy. The Native American way of "smudging" is one way to energetically cleanse places, so that we are not needlessly exposed to subtle energy pollution. Also, there are crystals capable of neutralizing certain energies, and Feng Shui—ancient wisdom/art of environmental harmony. It utilizes the knowledge of positive energy flow and fields that is created by placing a variety of objects (incl. furniture) in relation to each other, in very specific ways. It is often used to harmonize the physical environments of our most private spheres (homes and gardens), our offices, etc., with highly beneficial effects: For example, we find ourselves sleeping better, more focused or joyous, and less depressed or aggressive.

"The common denominator of healthful techniques rests on several basic questions. Does the technique bring us more in line with who we really are? Does it help us to become more in harmony with ourselves and our universe? If so, then that technique fosters healing. The degree to which it brings about harmony determines the quality of the healing and the speed at which it takes place."

O. Carl Simonton

HOLISTIC INTERVENTION (HEALING)

The foregoing chapter represents the holistic paradigm of Body, Mind, Spirit and Environment for the purpose of healing the relationship of these components and each person's relationship with the world. It is a complete system of thought—a world view—in that it includes where life comes from (God), what life is (original, purest energy directly from the "Source"), and what its purpose is (redemption by means of transcending our illusions or erroneous ways). **Wellness or health (physical, mental and spiritual) is an automatic, natural by-product when we fulfill this divine purpose, while dis-ease and distress result from doing anything else.** According to this holistic definition of good or ill health, both wellness and disease are God's indicators, inviting our conscious awareness to whether we are fulfilling our purpose or straying from it. The further we stray, the more pain and disaster will result.

All creation is viewed as one *live organism,* an interactive, dynamic system of energies with differing levels of density (vibratory rates/frequencies). These energies are capable of interacting in a multitude of ways. Apart from physical interaction, there is communication directly from Mind to Mind using our non-physical sensory organs (the Chakras), and "knowing" by means of intuition—the quantum approach to communication—from spirit spark to spirit spark. Coming from the same source, there is eternal inter-connectivity between all (pure) spirit. Utilizing this knowledge and approach gives us access to all there is to know.

Nothing dead or solid exists, only denser or less dense versions of one and the same energy which is life itself. Matter is merely "frozen" spirit—energy at its densest—but still capable to communicate, to interact, with the innate propensity (longing) to be *redeemed,* liberated or elevated in energy frequency. All energy is information and, therefore, intelligent and goal-directed.

A. DEFINITION OF HOLISTIC THERAPY

The holistic paradigm stresses *spiritual development* (returning to the source, the original state of energy) over any other goal. The alleviation of physical symptoms is not seen as paramount. Physical repairs are superficial and temporary if the will of the spirit remains ignored. Healing, then, consists of attending to the will of the spirit, i.e., the mental and emotional components preventing healthy spirit unfolding. Wellness is a natural by-product of developing toward spirit dominance, rather than being driven by self-made goals (ego coupled with the common, conscious mind) and a vast number of unconscious processes running amok. Development toward spirit dominance can be achieved *in the presence of disease and does not stop with one's physical death.* The holistic paradigm, then, is a marriage between mysticism and modern science, between the feminine and masculine, Yin and Yang.

The International Society for the Study of Subtle Energies and Energy Medicine calls the evolution of our new paradigm a combination of "Science and Inner Experience" (Sixth Annual Conference, 1996). For our health care, this means as much the masculine approach of *researching* and *doing—creating physical circumstances* conducive for good health—as it means the *omission,* **un**learning and **un**doing of harmful things. The latter approach might be considered a feminine one, naturally revealing the sacred, inherent goodness in all things which automatically blossoms in the proper environment. While the masculine approach is primarily based on a three-dimensional brain and the physical senses for the creation of physical changes, the feminine is focused on sensing dangers and the creation of non-physical circumstances (mental and emotional) by means of intuition and spiritual abilities (including blessing). All capabilities are present in all of us, men and women alike; unfortunately, they are not valued the same and manifested alike in our world today.

The holistic paradigm and, most certainly any model for good health care, is striking a balance between the two, within each of us, between the sexes, within and between countries. A successful marriage requires both to be equally actualized and valued. Nothing less can possibly constitute *Wholeness,* neither collectively nor individually. As long as we ridicule or even condemn (perhaps even in the name of God or the Bible) so-called *psychic* phenomena and capabilities, we are out of balance. If we do not believe that contact with the spirit world is possible (incl. angels, spirit guides, astrology, Tarot, Medicine Wheel, etc.), then we also do not believe that God can actually communicate with us, neither directly nor through our priests. As long as we call subjective, human experience (e.g., client's self-reports) *soft data* and then discount it for being *soft,* and as long as we favor *real* facts and *hard* sciences as the only *real* science, then it is little wonder that we will be miserable and, at the same time, be completely out of touch with it. In reality, our subjective experience of our lives is the only thing that really matters to anybody! If our subjective experience is discounted, we become miserable without conscious access to these impressions. Finally, our Mind has only one last resort to try to make itself known: Destruction of our physical "homes" (the body and the environment). This is exactly where we are today, i.e., vastly depressed and plagued by an untold number of stressors and dis-eases, in a world full of manmade *conveniences,* manmade *pleasures* and *material* abundance.

To derive a workable model from the holistic paradigm, for the purpose of holistic health care, we need to *define HOLISTIC THERAPY* as...:

ANY CONDITION THAT STRENGTHENS THE INHERENT SPIRIT, FITTED TO A PERSON'S CURRENT POINT OF SPIRITUAL DEVELOPMENT, SO THAT S/HE CAN TAKE THE NEXT STEP TOWARD SPIRIT DOMINANCE OVER ALL OTHER FACTORS INHERENT IN LIVING.

Holistic Therapy, then, is the intervention at any point in this system, *without harming any of the others,* thereby accepting the existence of subtle energy bodies and realms. As a side light, this idea is by no means new. Mention of subtle energy bodies can be found in writings emanating from a variety of cultures, through the ages, including in the Bible, from India to Greece and Egypt, and from European and American philosophers and theosophists (Thompson, K., 1996).

B. CLASSIFICATION OF HOLISTIC THERAPIES

Two aspects mark all therapies, i.e., their point of intervention and their goal or intended end point. Just as a drug prescribed to alleviate involuntary hand movements by modulating brain chemistry has a clear point of intercept (the brain) and an intended end point (the shaking hands), so do holistic therapies in our expanded model of human energy fields. If we classify therapies by their respective points of intervention/intended effect, we immediately are able to distinguish between body-oriented therapies as the one described, if the end goal is on the physical level; or spiritual therapies, if the goal of intervention is somewhere in the Mind. By "plugging in" a therapy into this model (Figure 2), we determine its direction in relation to the body, the Mind and/or spirit. We can determine related fields/therapies that support our intervention from either "side" (the denser or finer adjacent bodies/fields), and we can identify environmental changes conducive for healing.

All therapies become *Body-Therapies* if a practitioner's mindset and conscious end goal is to *repair the physical body.*

If physical repair is viewed as paramount—above all other components of wellness—then such a therapy is *not* holistic. In other words, the purpose for which a therapy is used ultimately determines its classification. Practitioners should advertise accordingly to not mislead the public.

Contrarily, all body therapies can be holistic if practitioners view them and themselves in the context of this enlarged, holistic paradigm:

A body therapy *is* holistic, if it takes into conscious consideration the will of the patient's spirit *and* subtle energy fields affected by the disorder and/or the intervention.

A holistic practitioner who tunes in to a patient's spirit will knows whether or not this patient may be helped by a particular therapy (or at all). At the latest, s/he will get the answer to this question when the therapy brings relief or persistently fails. When an ailment is stubborn or repeatedly recurs (sometimes it recurs in the form of some other, new ailment), then it is not the practitioner who is the failure. S/he *is* responsible, however, for recognizing additional components to the ailment and for referring this client appropriately.

A minimum consideration after surgery, for example, must be given to healing the affected energy fields. Inflicting a physical wound invariably injures the non-physical bodies as well. This is evidenced by the common experience that old scars/injuries suddenly hurt again when the person finally undergoes bio-energy therapy, even many years later. These wounds are felt /sensed in affected energy bodies in the area of the original injury. Reports usually indicate that the pain is "larger" than the actual scar or the affected organ, similar to a hang-over headache being perceived as "larger" than the head. These sensations always stop after one or two healing sessions, never to return, allowing the conclusion that energy healing of subtle body "tissue" has been achieved. Any injury in our subtle energy field represents a hole in our boundaries, rendering us vulnerable in some fashion.

Classification and identification of holistic therapies can take place by answering the following questions:

- Where in the model does the therapy *primarily* intercept (physical body, ether body, astral/mental/causal bodies or energy fields)? Example: Acupressure points in the foot.
- Where in the model does the goal-directed energy inherent in the intervention usually take effect? (Healers often do not know this. As we meditate on these questions, this door, too, will be opened unto us). In our example, it is the ether realm, by intensifying the contact and information flow from the etheric body to its more physical counterpart (through pressure). Concurrently, we temporarily "push" aside erroneous information in the affected etheric body, by means of our prayer, good intentions and unconditional love. We theorize that these positive energy impulses travel via meridians (which represent the etheric counterpart of our physical nervous system) to the affected area and alert or stimulate it. In this fashion, at a minimum, self-healing is facilitated or encouraged. We *must* theorize here to the best of our abilities, so that hypotheses can be formulated and tested.
- How does the therapy strengthen the spirit and support spirit dominance over all other factors inherent in living? (Only what is conscious can be voluntarily and deliberately subordinated to our inherent spirit). Example: Acupressure does not, in and by itself, involve the patient's conscious awareness. However, memories and "themes" may emerge as a result of this therapy. This means that other subtle energy bodies are involved, with the issues to be addressed in the form of counseling/conversation and/or other suitable therapy.
- How do I do it? Example: I *mindfully* (with the therapeutic goal in mind) apply pressure to said points. This is a double application of energy, i.e., contact with the patient directly from Mind to Mind via the mutual goal and purpose of the therapy, coupled with the exact physical pressure.
- Major benefits? Be specific, based on your experience, e.g., improved sleep/relaxation/appetite. In our example, perhaps it is improved liver functioning.

The goal and benefit of such classification is to, hopefully, arrive at a Manual for Holistic Therapies, similar to the manual for (body-oriented) *Alternative Medicine—The Definitive Guide,* compiled by the Burton Goldberg Group (1993). This will help therapists clarify for clients how they work, considering that the same technique placed in different hands or used by different therapists' Minds might change the point of effectiveness, dependent upon individual practitioner differences of intention and capabilities. Further, by *mapping* the therapies *in relation to each other,* this should facilitate an easier referral system and choice of therapies complementing any one healer's particular intervention.

> Mapping holistic therapies is easier for some techniques than others. For example, subtle energy therapy has as its goal to take effect exactly where the root cause disharmony is located. This can be *any* of the non-physical realms. It is always the highest (least dense) level on which the disorder/disharmony is manifest. For long-standing, chronic, and degenerative physical disorders this is typically the causal plane. However, not every practitioner working with subtle energies is capable to influence this level, by means of personal, developmental attributes. In other words, classification of therapies can be a complex issue, complicated by *differences by disorder treated* and *variability in therapist ability.* Furthermore, the healing process may differ from client to client due to their unique need for pace and sequence of unraveling their particular blockage or error. However, recognizing that classification may be complicated, does not mean it is impossible. Generalities can be extracted that are usually, generally, most of the time true, regardless of the variable factors. For subtle energy therapy, the definition of the end goal simply is, "The highest, finest subtle energy field on which the disorder is manifest."
>
> Most likely, additional classification methods will be forthcoming to account for some remaining variability. Also, there are *always* qualitative differences between any two practitioners (including physicians), even if they share the same title, graduated from the same school or even had the same GPA. Some are simply more effective than others, and each offers qualities some patients cherish but others do not.

C. EXAMPLES OF COMBINED HOLISTIC INTERVENTION SCENARIOS

In addition to the "minimum consideration after surgery" mentioned above, the following suggests other possible, combined *holistic* intervention scenarios:

1. Bone Fracture

- Physical/medical intervention: Straighten, connect and support severed bone. Apply cast.
- Ether, astral and mental field healing (referral to a subtle-energy therapist).
- Concurrent holistic counseling: Address these questions: "Why did this happen to me?" "What is my arm/finger/leg... trying to tell me—what am I trying to tell myself?" "How am I hindering my arm/finger/leg... from functioning properly?"
- Environmental adjustments, if applicable: Creating a safer, accident-free home or office.

2. Emergence of painful memories/life experiences

- Aid full recollection by means of Chakra Therapy, (past life) regression therapy, crystal therapy. etc.
- Holistic Counseling: Focus on learning about one's unconscious and the learning content *for the soul*: "What is the jewel hidden in the experience?" "How does this experience strengthen and stretch me beyond my current limits?" Practicing forgiveness ("letting go").
- Humanistic psychotherapy: Grief and anger work. Finishing the "incomplete Gestalt" or similar action to heal relationships, if applicable (making amends; letter writing/burning; confrontation with involved persons).
- Support healing of the soul's "unconscious" learning by means of Bach Flower Remedies or similar essences.

3. Chronic Disorders

- Medical diagnosis and alleviation of immediate symptoms to a bearable level. Note: No mindful exploration of underlying issues will occur while the patient suffers extreme physical distress!
- Support physical healing of afflicted organs/tissue by means of one or more of the suited therapies for this purpose, e.g., color therapy, fasting/nutrition, herbal therapies, etc.
- Metaphysical *interpretation* of symptoms followed by holistic counseling aimed at the conscious exploration of underlying themes, e.g., through Holographic Repatterning. Note however, that all long-term, chronic illness involves *all* subtle energy levels, including the Causal. At least one practitioner involved in the

team must be able to reach and modulate the patient's Causal Body.

- Support counseling and emotional and mental healing with meditation, energy work, movement and aroma therapies, and/or other therapies suited for that purpose.
- Together with the patient, identify needed lifestyle changes, based on clients' own insight and self-recognition, e.g., nutrition, environmental harmonizing (eliminating stresses where possible; adding sources for joy and wherever possible; Feng Shui; reassessing electromagnetic pollution, e.g., relocating the computer and/or protecting self by means of crystals, removing the TV set from the bedroom), new career goals, relationships, and so on.

For more ideas and information on *The Healer-Physician Team,* please consult *Light Emerging* (Brennan, B.A., 1993).

The choice of therapy/ies largely depends on what a client is open to and on what is available and affordable. *All* holistic therapies have the propensity to heal, as long as they are administered with unconditional love, free of judgment of the client *and* of the illness. As is the case for the choice from among the many conventional psychotherapies, *holistic practitioners, too, use what works for a particular client.* Additionally, we check where in the holistic wellness model each therapy intercepts and intends to take effect. Under no circumstances will the client's free will be circumvented or subjugated.

If this were a world of cooperative spirit between all practitioners, with nothing but the patient's welfare in mind, instead of so many jealously guarding their *turfs,* we could all treat the patient concurrently, right from the start. What difference does it make who or what ultimately healed the patient, so long as s/he heals?! Health care can neither be about blame and failure nor about praise and awards. A truly cooperative spirit in such a combined healing approach can greatly add to the healing *environment* a patient needs. When we put our Minds together in a kindred atmosphere and eliminate all other motives from each, chances for healing can only improve, because of the healing environment created by such kindred spirit alone.

D. IMPLICATIONS FOR HOLISTIC PRACTITIONERS

1. This is true for any holistic approach to wellness: The client assumes full responsibility for their own distress as well as the

recovery from it, and makes informed choices based on the available information and their current, conscious values and believe system. The client understands that no healer guarantees a *specific* outcome. Each person heals differently and at their own, unique pace. Thereby, healing is the most individualistic and personal affair under the sun. While all body-therapies aim at achieving physical changes, spiritual therapies view physical changes *subordinate* to spiritual wellness/harmony, i.e., making peace with one's lot. Sometimes this may mean helping the patient and their families make peace with death.

2. All drugs (and foods!) deliver information to the body. Always consider if the drug addresses actual causes. Of course, a patient must be moved beyond immediate, physical danger or suffering. However, if a drug does not help in making unconscious processes conscious or actively prevents conscious awareness (e.g., by rendering the patient too drugged to think and feel or by eliminating any and all physical motivation to think about the disorder at all), the necessary attitudinal change is not forthcoming. Then the drug is most likely *enabling* the maintenance of an unhealthy attitude and, therefore, actually harmful in the long run. Remember: It is an *attitudinal change* that constitutes the actual healing.

3. The same principle applies to any other form of therapy: Does it provide an *escape*—just another *excuse*—for the patient to continue to avoid his/her inner dilemma or conflict? Then the therapy will fail, at best; or it will cause more harm than good, at worst. Always consider what the effect of your work might be on the patient's overall Mind, other than the point of intercept of your therapy.

4. Never work with a patient to whom you feel an aversion or inner resistance which you are unable to put aside for the time of treatment. *Your* Mind affects the patient more than you think and has everything to do with whether or not healing will indeed be facilitated.

5. Always start, finish and accompany your work with *prayer*: "Thy will, not mine be done. Amen." Do not accept credit *or* blame for the outcome.

6. By now, a psychotherapist will understand that there is no such thing as a *hallucination*. There is no such thing as *not* being *in focus*. When we are not focused on the physical realm, we are automatically focused on another. The impressions gained on other realms present opportunities for patients to grow by taking conscious charge of

their Minds. Obviously, this will never happen if we do not take their impressions seriously. It is also a challenge to health professionals to learn about other realms (and their own resistance to and problems with these), too—vicariously, if you will. In fact, these phenomena have always presented the scientific community with the unique opportunity to expand its horizons. Unfortunately, this opportunity has gone vastly unused and responded to by hushing the impressions up, e.g., stopping our conscious awareness of them by means of drug "therapy," instead of learning to mindfully reject the *intruders*.

7. Similarly, caution must be used to label patients as *hypochondriacs* (in the sense of *imagining illness*). Often, these are patients who are sensitive to disharmonies in their subtle energy bodies, despite all conditioning to ignore those. The reported discomfort is information that could and should be utilized in healing, i.e., treat the energy bodies first and foremost, before *accusing* a client of *desiring* to be ill. When people hurt, the last thing they need is be insulted by judgmentalness.

8. The holistic wellness model is a complete school of thought for psychotherapy, i.e., *holistic* psychotherapy or counseling. It is a *Theory of Personality* more complete than any I studied in graduate school. The graphical illustrations actually *place* the Mind (personality or psyche), including its emotional, thinking and intuiting components, conscious awareness and the unconscious, purpose/motivation, and the ego, *in relation to the physical body* and to each other. They are not just symbolic representations of abstract constructs like *The Adult* speaking with *The Child,* as in Transactional Analysis, or the Id/Ego/Superego circle in Freudian psychoanalysis. Furthermore, the holistic system is larger, more encompassing and, therefore, more "whole" than all models currently in use, in that they include *all* human experiencing, instead of specifically *excluding* religious feelings or even labeling *paranormal* experiences as pathological. Finally, it places the human being in relation to all of creation.

All psychotherapies have—more or less unwittingly—been dealing with subtle energy realities, i.e., on *verbalizing* about mental and emotional components to wellness, which happen to be housed in subtle energy bodies/fields. How much more effective these therapies can be when dealing with these realms in a more consciously aware and purposive fashion! Also, those therapies based on a developmental model, i.e., on virtually unlimited *learning,* have been *approximating* holism all along without, however, addressing the issue of, "Who or what in us learns from whom or what"? When the focus is consciously and expressly on *spirit unfolding/dominance* in each individual, whereby the less *spirited* (energetically denser) components *learn* from the inherent and surrounding spirit, then we have a *holistic psychotherapy.*

9. The *placebo effect* is a myth. When healing occurs in conjunction with treatment—whether as part of a treatment or control group—the patient has received *something* to which s/he responded favorably. The healing agent may not be the drug or specific treatment tried/tested on the patient. However, obviously, the patient is reacting to something that is—more or less inadvertently—also administered along with the specific treatment. A kind word, attention, environmental influences as light, colors, harmonious arrangement and choice of furniture, cleanliness, music/sound/tranquillity or the mere change of scenery (being away from home)...all may act as a healing agent, if not *the* healing agent a patient needed. Furthermore, there are the mental causes, e.g., the patient's simply having made up his/her mind to finally get help now, which is why the patient is in the treatment room today (but was not yesterday); plus subtle energy fields of the helper(s)...any of these could set the very energy impulse that *jump-starts* the patient's *car,* i.e., triggers the mind/body to resume self-healing.

The only exception to this may be the normal progression of a disorder, self-healing already being in progress, reaching its natural conclusion shortly after or during treatment. In other words, this concerns people who would have overcome their malady anyhow, without treatment of any kind, during the same amount of time. The so-called spontaneous recoveries we will never quite sort out and know about, concerning *any* type of research experiment. It is often said about Dr. Freud that, during the average time frame it took for his psychoanalysis, most if not all patients would have naturally overcome their condition, without *any* treatment. We will never know if those who seek help belong to the same population that recovers naturally and *spontaneously* and who have been used as a statistical baseline to determine *average progression* and *spontaneous recovery* for various disorders. Since spontaneous recoveries/self-healing can occur for *any* disorder ever studied and cannot completely be controlled for in *any* study, I believe their small numbers can be ignored in holistic health care studies as well. It would indeed be a highly curious coincidence if there were a great many people who so happen to reach the final stage of their disorder and get well by themselves just as they enter treatment! More likely, they experience and respond to a healing agent of some sort during treatment.

WHAT AGENT IS BENEFICIAL TO WHOM is *the* question to be researched and answered. All discussions about *placebo-effects* are futile and have only one purpose: To stall the investigation and to draw the helper, research and/or treatment into question. They add absolutely nothing to answering any of the questions we really need to answer. Therefore, again: A *placebo-effect does not exist,* just as *nothing cannot exist,* by definition. An *effect* always has a *cause.* There is no effect ever in the absence of a cause. I hope that, going forward, everyone of you will confront and stop cold anyone engaging in such nonsensical and nothing but negatively motivated placebo-rhetoric.

10. At one point or another in all holistic therapies, the issue of *loathing* and *self-loathing* must be addressed. Loathing is, to some extent and in some fashion, *always* involved at the root of disharmony. To place a negative value judgment on anything in God's creation means to be at odds with God. This is, by definition, a *fall from grace,* from harmony or balance. It is counter-directed to life itself and the source for disharmonious, erroneous thoughts and emotions which then cause pain and suffering, eventually involving one's physical health. People who loathe poison themselves and their environment. They become a highly contagious virus or cancer in the universe. We must reject such erroneous thinking and feeling, along with the resulting behaviors, without loathing the *patient,* the *carrier* of the virus, or the virus itself. If we do not reject someone's loathing of us, we become infected. We begin to loathe, too; usually ourselves, which is loathing turned inward. There is no lasting recovery or healing without reversing one's negative valuing and, thereby, undoing the chain reaction of disharmony on all levels. We want to learn to *deflect* lovelessness, i.e., loathing, *short of loathing it*! Holistic practitioners can be instrumental in facilitating this learning process.

E. HEURISTIC VALUE FOR RESEARCH AND SCIENCE

The possibilities and implications of the holistic health model for scientific research are virtually endless. By specifying the point of intercept and the intended impact point of a therapy, correlational studies can be conducted and evaluated to this effect. This should aid research to test for much more specific effects than heretofore possible. Allow healers to tell researchers what the expected effects might be! For body therapies, physical effects of the therapy can be observed fairly directly. For changes in the astral and mental fields, there are powerful psychological tests to assess *attitudinal changes,* before and after treatment. Additionally, results can be correlated with clairvoyants' and the healers' intuitive observations and impressions. We cannot predict what new tools and techniques may come out of this, as well as new scientific realms and *measurable realities.* All scientific disciplines (outside bio-medical research) are sure to be involved in the measurement of subtle energies and their various manifestations, in human and other organisms, for application in so-called hard and soft sciences, in ecological decisions and how we live our lives, individually and collectively. Expanding our horizon in this fashion can only add a deeper meaning to all our lives, and everything that adds meaning—*real* meaning—contributes to wellness.

F. THE LEGAL AND POLITICAL ENVIRONMENTS OF HOLISM

I encourage practitioners everywhere to individually reflect and to get together, compare notes and to streamline their concepts, definitions, descriptions and language used therefore, in order to compile a classification system for holistic therapies. There is great potential benefit to our total health care, more precise information for users and other practitioners, and to stimulate related research. Understandably, many holistic practitioners are reluctant to come forward for this work in the present legal, professional and political environment. However, professional organizations, politicians and even many patients can not properly relate to holistic health care due to the many scattered and half-way concealed activities everywhere (refer back to Part I: Amazing Contradictions, if necessary). Finally, holistic practitioners themselves have great difficulty relating to each other, because they do not necessarily use the same nomenclature. Most certainly, laws and political views never change themselves. It takes many people to courageously and actively work at effecting change. The consumer/patient is not likely to effect this change—how could they ever be more convinced of what holistic practitioners know and do than these practitioners themselves?

The utility of the holistic paradigm and model for holistic health care, then, is to facilitate and foster a positive, cooperative relationship and climate between all concerned. Streamlining holistic therapies along *one* definition each of wellness and dis-ease, and *one* definition of holistic intervention, using *one common language*, will help resolve much of the current confusion and mistrust. Practitioners are encouraged to agree on specific, well-defined designations of their skill which mean something to everybody, i.e., identify their skill as, indeed, *holistic;* differentiate between body, spiritual and environmental therapies, holistic psychotherapy/counseling and diagnostic methods (for subtle energy disorders which may or may not yet be manifest on the physical level) which may not be therapies in and by themselves. Ideally, this is done by all answering the same set of questions for a common format.

As a consequence of good definitions and streamlining, terms like *counseling, therapy, treatment, healing, medicinal, intervention, prevention, diagnosis, prognosis,* etc., will have to become vastly *de-regulated.* Over-regulation and certain professional interest groups' claiming ownership of such common terms and each practitioner's jealously guarding his/her particular little piece of *truth* only prevents the one and only truth. It prevents health because, in the end, there is only one health, but the pieces of the puzzle cannot come together.

May this book's streamlining effort stimulate cooperation in the scientific, professional, legal and political communities. We can not remain separate communities if we are to serve humankind, i.e., each other, including ourselves. Until open-minded cooperation happens, *none* of us will be a model of wellness in the sense of honesty, openness, congruency, unselfish motivation and *healthy* pride in what we do.

"Rather than the earth and sky being equal, which is evident in many creation myths, for some reason the sky became dominant, represented by the superiority of the [common] mind and intellect."

Lynne Morgan

BRIDGING THE MODELS

Healing can be one of the most natural processes on earth, *if only we let it happen*! Nature inherently knows how to heal itself, to include our bodies and Minds. The masculine mindset and a patriarchal science continuously attempt to make these processes endlessly complicated, in that they aim at *objectifying* a highly personalized, subjective happening. The feminine, instead, merely acts as a facilitator, with healing being the responsibility, activity and personal experience of the client. Facilitation of healing begins, simply, with tuning our Mind in to clients' Minds, and not by a myriad of clichés and scientific dogmas, charts and graphs, that allegedly *prove* that we really know something.

To play on a popular saying, "Healing Happens," whether we know how or not. We need to scientifically "understand" how healing works as much or as little as we need be consciously aware of every heartbeat. Healers are very happy when some of what they do becomes measurable and, thereby, *fact* to otherwise skeptical others. However, if such research is not forthcoming, they cannot and will not lose faith in what they do and know. Healers are interested in information that can be validated by our subjective life experience. In fact, to the feminine in all of us, the commonly accepted/expected, *objective* and *intellectualized* ways often appear as *obstacles* to finding the very truth. Therefore, healers are little impressed by scientific clichés, especially if these are used to intimidate. No one likes to learn from someone who intimidates (although many of us have spent many years studying *conventional* approaches)—it makes one wonder if what is taught adds anything of *value* and *meaning* to one's life. No one likes to be in the presence of arrogance. Such encounters are on the expense of one's self-esteem, dignity and belief in one's own abilities. None of this is healthy and, therefore, to be avoided by anyone in the health professions. The biggest insult to the feminine in all of us, but especially to healers (and to God), is to attach the negative label of *irrationality* to a healer's most precious gift—*intuition.* For more information on femininity, please read Lynne Morgan's excellent essay, "Women and the Goddess Today," in *Paganism Today* (Harvey G.& Hardman, C., Eds., 1996).

Again, a healer's activities are feminine in that they consist of *un*-doing or temporarily setting aside the conditions that make the person sick—mentally, emotionally, spiritually and in the spiritual environment. This is in direct opposition to what medical doctors do, i.e., doing or adding something to the organism which counteracts physical and chemical components of the disorder. Healing, instead, is *passive*—it merely *allows* nature to take its natural course, *by omitting that which makes sick or introduces disharmony to the system.* In an unconditionally loving setting, clients are safe to drop defense mechanisms and hence to explore just *how* they have been making or keeping themselves sick. Only huge doses of love create the atmosphere in which consciousness can venture into previous blind spots, tapping into information that was previously suppressed because of its threatening content. Of all factors known to healers today, the absence of fear is more healing than anything else while, conversely, fear and anxiety probably contribute the greatest share to most if not all our distress. Unconditional love is *the* antidote to anxieties and fears so prevalent in patriarchal systems.

Healing is, then, that which takes place all by itself, under the proper conditions. It is not something a *healer does* but, rather, an automatic response to an omission of negative influences, in the presence of love. Healing is accomplished not by the healer, but by the helee and nature. This is the reason why every client may respond differently to the same holistic intervention. It is also the reason why healers are much less interested in *how healing works,* because it is something accomplished by the *client.* Instead, we are interested in *what prevents healing.* Furthermore, we are only *secondarily* interested in so many viruses or medical diagnoses. Instead, the *location* of the disorder in the body or Mind is of greater interest, as every body part, organ or energy field has an expressed *function* in the person's organism. Which part or organ *under-functions* (or over-functions) can be seen, then, as an expression of this person's under-functioning or over-functioning as an entity in a much larger organism. This is how we can derive the metaphysical interpretations of disorders and of so many medical diagnoses. However, how each person recovers is a very personal and private affair. No two people respond identically to identical treatments for identical diagnoses, since no two people have *exactly* identical issues with similar stimuli or circumstances which contributed to the disorder.

Also, no two people ever start out with exactly the same knowledge and resources or learn at exactly the same speed.

I need not know so much about nature's inherently normal and harmonious processes, except so not to inadvertently upset them. Even mystical prophesy—like medical diagnoses and prognoses—does not come about until something seems to be taking a turn in the wrong direction. How my heart makes itself beat is of little interest to anybody until it suddenly beats irregularly. The questions which medicine asks at that point is, "What can *I do* to *make* it start or pump regularly again"; "The system *needs something,* which must be *added* to it." It is a theory of disorder resulting from a *lack* or *omission.* The healer's view is directly opposite to this in that disorder is viewed as a result of an *over-abundance of something negative,* which *must be omitted,* whether this is five cups of coffee a day or abundant negative thoughts and emotions. Aiding the healing process, corresponding information can be fed to the organism, all aimed at stimulating the will and ability to recognize and omit that which prevents, through insight, for the sake of self-love. Holistic therapies use gentle, non-intrusive facilitators of such learning—neither of which bypass an individual's free will/consciousness. These may consist of herbs, nutrition, energy (as color, sound, bio-energy, pressure, crystals, etc.) applied or delivered to all the right places, and all aim to serve the purpose of facilitating learning about disharmony and disorderliness. Health, joy, goodness and beauty, then, are things that naturally and automatically bubble up and take over if we omit disorderliness, disharmony and ugliness as a result of genuine learning and a voluntary, lasting change of *attitude(s),* rather than just some outward *behavior* change. Behavior changes *not* coupled with learning will always only be *temporary.*

In our world today, constructed by man, we are no longer in a naturally harmonious environment. We are bombarded with externalities of manmade systems and products which have assumed self-propelling properties. As such, they are vastly beyond most individuals' control or influence. We no longer *just* have *normal* earth and solar radiation and bacteria to respond to which our natural organism is vastly equipped to handle. Where it was not, western medicine stepped in and came up with some truly remarkable interventions. But that was then. Today, we deal primarily with *man-made disorders.* Such disorders include but are not limited to: Drug side-effects and drug interaction; the high rate of iatrogenic disease (induced by some treatment or diagnostic procedure, in doctors' offices and hospitals); allergies and malnutrition due to unhealthy food, caused by modern cultivation, presentation and preservation methods, genetic engineering and other fads (fat-free "fat," caffeine-free "coffee," sugarless "sweets," etc.); reactions to high levels of toxins in our water and in the environment; accidents caused by manmade machines, including cars, and all stress-related disorders. Since *we made these dangers,* we must re-ascertain our reasons for making them, to then—hopefully—choose to omit some of them.

Ultimately, this means a combination of the two approaches. On the one hand, we need masculine *doing,* for quickly moving a patient beyond life-threatening dangers (e.g., re-starting the heart, stilling the bleeding, bandaging the open wound, emergency surgery, reducing the fever, etc.). For emergency interventions and acute, physical illness, western medicine remains unsurpassed in the world! While the power of prayer is not to be underestimated, in general, feminine approaches are particularly ill-equipped for emergency situations. On the other hand, we need the feminine approaches, too, for helping patients recover *after* emergency interventions, and also for helping them learn about what to omit in case of chronic disorders and stresses of all kinds, using the "gentle facilitators" mentioned above. For environmental considerations (e.g., subtle energy components in the environment and physical safety measures) all of us can put our heads and hearts together. In this fashion, we achieve a marriage between science and mysticism, between the masculine and the feminine in our culture and world. We add a matriarchal system to the current patriarchal one, side by side. It almost goes without saying that, for this marriage to work, both forces and strivings must be equal. No one system or therapy is inherently better or the *only one*. Equality means that we learn to distinguish *when* to use *which,* without personal prejudice. Just because anger may have worked well for someone in some past situations, this does not mean that is the only good response or the most effective response in *all* situations and for all people. And so it is with therapies, models, and all theories. They probably all have their applications; all are *true* in some cases. The challenge consists of determining which applies to which situation.

Prejudice exists in many ways. Patriarchy is a system of power, silently agreed upon and maintained by all parties, which determines "Who gets to want. ...We all agree to do this dance together, and changing the steps disturbs all of us. ...Most of us, myself included, don't like to think about our own unconscious cooperation with patriarchy" (Horst, E.A., 1996). Patriarchally-oriented men and women must learn to tolerate, respect and heed being told to stop or undo so many things, whether or not they fully *understand,* and they must stop trying to intimidate femininity into masculine dogmas and regimen, e.g., jargon and the very means of inquiry and definition of "valid" questions and "good" or "worthwhile" strivings and desires. These can no longer be determined by patriarchal systems *alone*. Women have been studying masculine values, techniques and systems, in order to communicate with men—to perhaps *reach* them and *be heard* one day. Instead, these systems have become ever less communicable, less accurate, more rigid and arrogant. With it, love (the main but most mystical of all healing agents) and wellness are disappearing. The feminine in all of us has allowed and enabled this development. Intuition and spiritual gifts have been reduced to and abused for *codependency* (all codependent individuals have heightened psychic abilities and are extremely good at "reading Minds," for example, at "reading between the lines," anticipating events and sensing people's conscious and unconscious motivations, moods, and so on). Furthermore, virtues such as kindness, tolerance, openness and gentleness have come to be viewed as an invitation for abuse and rape, if not as downright *reckless* and *stupid.* When Christian virtues (which include psychic/spiritual abilities, as Christ himself is our *model psychic*) are *subordinated* and *sacrificed,* then those blessed with such virtues and abilities will be used to *enable* non-spiritual agendas. In addition, they are scorned and/or ridiculed. It is, therefore, our joint responsibility to create the mutual respect necessary to facilitate a *holistic* paradigm expansion, consisting of patriarchal *and* matriarchal specialties. Compressing matriarchal wisdom *into* a patriarchal paradigm is neither possible nor would it represent a paradigm shift or expansion. Let us start by accepting and acknowledging that so much is not "researchable" and "solvable" in the "old" ways. Much of creation can simply not be comprehended by intellectualizing.

This is the time for the re-awakening *and* dominance of the *spirit,* the spirit in all of us, not just men or just women. It is the time for re-introducing *awe* and *intuition, passion* (without confusing it for anger) and *compassion* (without confusing it for weakness). Nothing less will do. Nothing less will *heal.* Short of the capacity of awe, there is no more joy, love, gentleness, respect, tolerance, gratitude and (individual and social) wellness. Wellness largely depends on the presence of these virtues and capabilities, as a counter-balance to fear and competition, and as a resource reservoir in times of hardship and grief. The connection between awe and health needs not be proven scientifically. We have all the proof we need by looking around and within, by dragging ourselves out of bed and off to work every day, into the loveless traffic, smile-less supermarkets and back home to frustrated, depressed, angry or sick family members, and *feeling absolutely miserable and powerless* about it. What more proof does anybody need to "know for sure"? What if the corresponding research is never conducted?

Do we all have to die first? Who will be left to "*really* know," *then*?

There are many ways of knowing things, whereby the intuitive approaches can prove valuable and useful to stimulate and/or augment the current, scientific approach:

1. Intuition bypasses our currently, conscious and therefore highly limited thinking. It attempts to go straight to the source. It is neither influenced by one's own nor by anybody else's unconscious which forever waters down scientific experiments. Researchers can only establish *statistical* controls, for *consciously known* variables (usually, only *some* of these).

2. Intuition *is* inherently logical in that it does not argue with logic. It does not make itself true by means of its own definitions or other rationalizations. It simply *is* and does not rationalize at all. It does not worry about either/or questions. In holism, the answer is usually "Both" or, "It depends," resulting in a proper *sequencing* of instructions (instructions as to *when which* answer might apply), rather than arriving at singular, *mutually exclusive* answers. If a question is not answered, the riddle simply does not exist, at least not in the way it was posed. "What is true here?" is the issue, and not, "Is it logical and always true?" Think about it: Is it really logical to expect that *anything* would *always* be true, regardless of the situation?

For those of us currently without immediate, intuitive access, techniques exist and can be rehearsed to hone intuition. Such approaches include meditation, dreams, astrology, Tarot, channeling, and pendulum dowsing. Any raising of eyebrows at this point is, in and by itself, evidence of arrogance and discrimination, the very prejudice and imbalance mentioned above. As long as such discrimination is condoned, then the most virtuous among us may inadvertently support and unconsciously cooperate with patriarchy.

However, bridging the various models into one encompassing, holistic paradigm is much more than a merely *bi*-polar matter of patriarchy and matriarchy. A truly *holistic* paradigm accommodates more than the therapeutic models prevalent in the North-Western hemisphere. Holistic health care means *global* health care, across cultural and geographical divides, *without prejudice*. Practitioners of all therapies are asked to relate their model(s) to others and, with it, to one comprehensive Whole. The holistic paradigm stimulates and embraces this development by eliminating prejudice, e.g., the prejudice inherent in an over-valuation of *North-Western* science, methodology and medicine over all other knowledge.

Demonstrating the masculine and feminine forces within each of us, nourished by "the sky" above and "the earth" below," we arrive at the picture in Figure 6. In this drawing (as well as in Fig. 5), the human Chakra system is shown *facing* us, so that the person's right body half is on the left side. Note that the polarization is not merely *two*-fold in a multi-dimensional world. Polarization occurs between anything we split into two parts by means of our Mind. The two parts of anything we divide, for whatever purpose, begin to relate to each other in a polarized fashion. Mentally splitting a person into two halves vertically, results in a masculine-feminine polarization between the person's right and left body halves. Applying the division horizontally results in a similar polarization between the upper and lower body halves. We could continue any number of "splits" and forever find the same polarization, but let's limit our discussion here to the four most practical and observable ones.

Some "masculine" energy enters our system through the Crown Chakra, flowing downward, while some "feminine" energy enters through the Base Chakra from below. Within one and the same Chakra system, the organism circulates much of this energy around. It is used and funneled through the Chakra System into other dimensions, resulting in all our physical, emotional and mental activities. Masculine and feminine energy's traveling along our spine, initiates a particular pattern of *Chakra rotation.* Under healthy conditions, this rotation is as shown in Figure 6a.

In a holistic paradigm, then, one of the two snakes of the medical caduceus is *reversed,* as a symbol of health. The number of "loops" around the "axis" (here the axis is the spine; in the medical symbol, it is the mercury staff) is a fixed number seven, due to the seven main Chakras, whereas the medical caduceus is portrayed with varying numbers of "loops"). Further, the system is *open to other realms,* above and below and, of course, through the Chakras themselves. This symbol recurs in other cultures (and systems) as well, sometimes referred to as the *Serpent Fire* or *Kundalini.* Also, please note the resemblance between this picture and the well-known Yin/Yang Symbol.

Kundalini is usually described as two snakes, both climbing upward. **This one-directionality is due to an over-emphasis of "the sky" over "the earth,"** which then *becomes* our reality. However, evolution is *not* one-directional. God inhales and exhales simultaneously and continuously. In the fashion of *Jacob's Ladder,* spirit continues to descend and ascend, all at the same time. Creation *and* redemption are an *ongoing* process.

Across the globe, within each culture, *feminine* and *masculine* systems and knowledge exist. The medical science itself can be viewed with

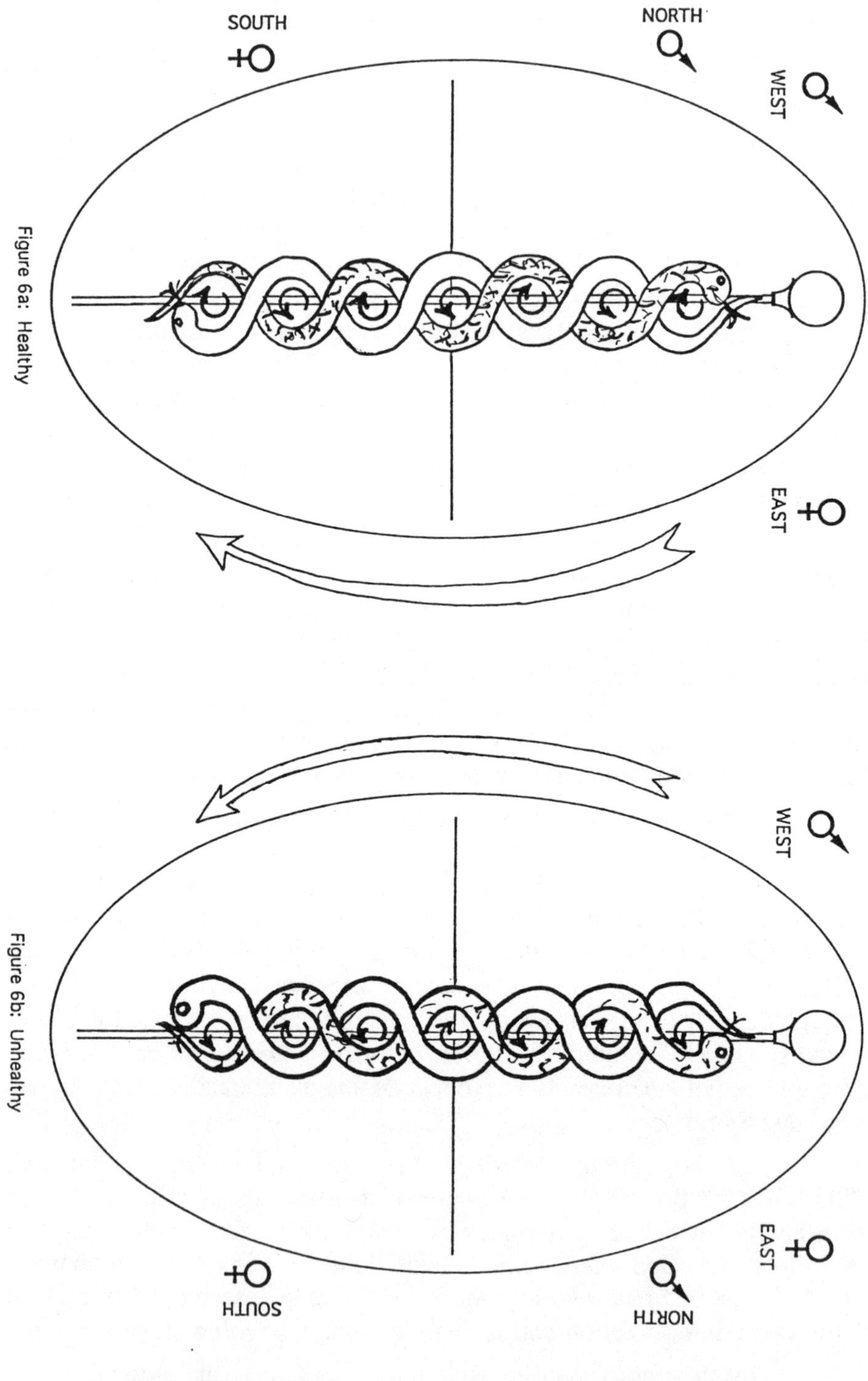

Figure 6: Femininity, Masculinity and Chakra Rotation

its feminine and masculine components, inasmuch as many drugs contain (or meanwhile simulate) natural herbal substances, knowledge of medicinal uses of *herbs being the oldest and most earthy/feminine of all medicines* and the scalpel and surgery representing the most masculine. Comparing western medicine with other disciplines in the Americas, since the arrival of Europeans here, its feminine counterpart has been Native American practices. *Native American healing can be viewed as feminine* when compared with medical science, as it relies on an intimate knowledge of the earth and *earth*-bound spirits, herbs and intuition (vision quests, psychic abilities of Medicine Men and Women, etc.). It goes without saying which of the two models dominates. Other cultures are sure to have their own masculine-feminine imbalances. Notwithstanding such imbalances, Figure 7 illustrates some major global trends in health care. **As America, like no other country, is the home for people from all cultures and countries, this is the place to build the bridge and balance everything into one comprehensive paradigm.** This is also the place to voluntarily reduce prejudice, by somewhat lowering the pedestal of (medical) science and, thereby, make way for a bit more love, intuition, nature, joy and awe. Then, perhaps, the miracles we so desperately need, e.g., to fix our health care crisis, may begin to happen, once again.

Globally, in a counter-clockwise, mental sweeping motion, our prevailing value systems were carried into the world. In its path were developing countries, China, Japan and, meanwhile, Russia, who replaced many of their own healing methods with north-western ones. China so embraced western science and medicine that it temporarily outlawed but later reinstated their own, ancient methods (Moyers, B., 1993). If not as radical as it happened with Native American culture, whatever we touch in the rest of the world seems to be inclined to surrender its unique spirit for the sake of Coca Cola, McDonald, quick-fixes and profit, whereby western knowledge (science and medicine) are among the most precious, tradable commodities.

Counter-clockwise-directed mental activity is not healthy for us humans. Indeed, most people who come to me for Chakra Therapy, initially arrive with their Crown and Root Chakras turning counter-clockwise. Usually, the Solar Plexus is also affected. This kind of *Chakra Disorder* seems to be an epidemic and symptomatic of some very prevalent but erroneous attitudes (Table 3, below, summarizes the effects of attitudes on Chakra rotation). Unfortunately, when we are stuck in this mode, the organism can no longer accept help, neither from above nor from below. I hypothesize that this erroneous rotation is the result of a conscious awareness which is predominantly located in the masculine-masculine quadrant,

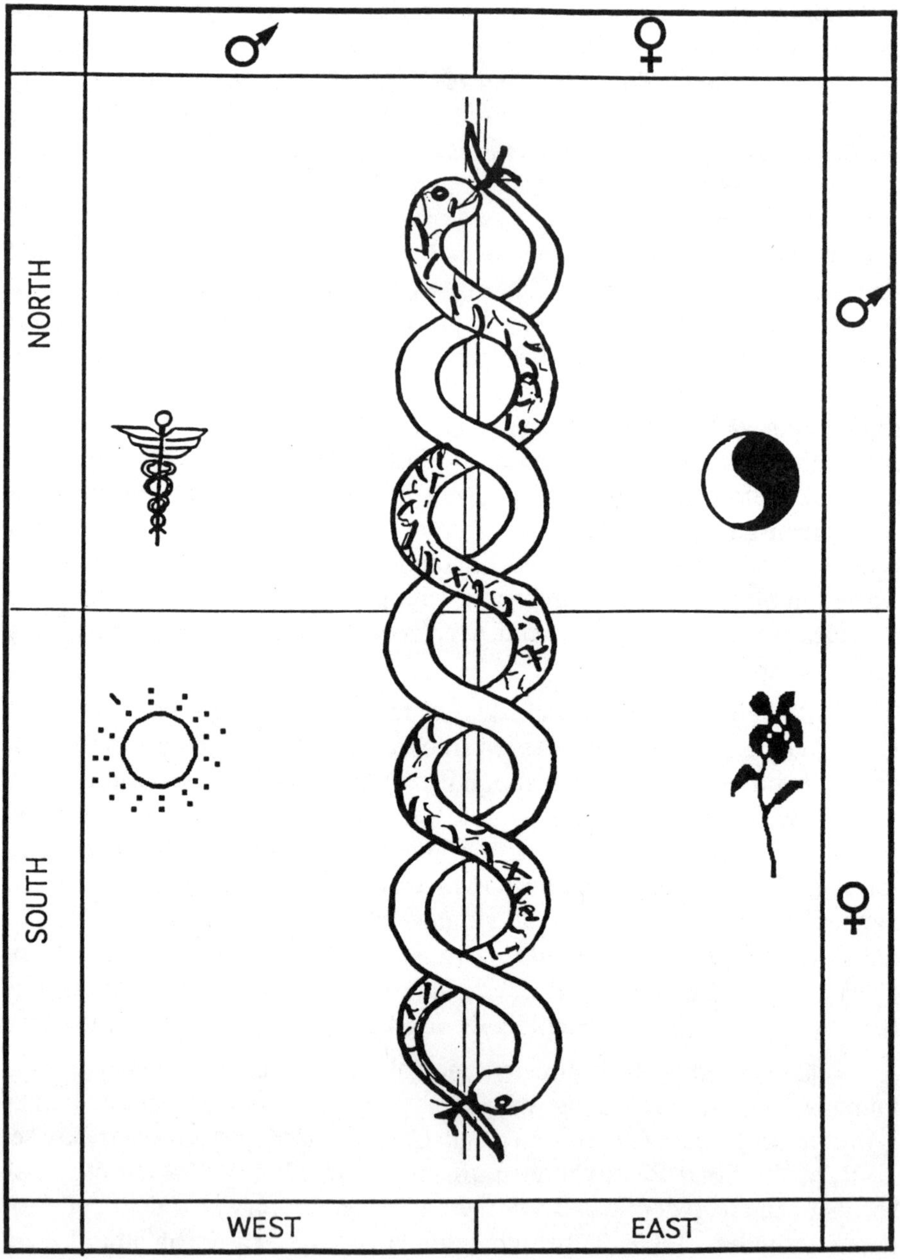

Figure 7: Global Health Care

CHAKRA	HEALTHY		UNHEALTHY	
	Rotation	Mode/Attitude	Rotation	Mode/Attitude
Crown	Clockwise	Unconditional sense of self or being: "I AM."	Counter-Clockwise	Sense of self or being is contingent upon certain conditions and circumstances: "Perhaps I *will* be, if only... ."
Brow	Counter-Clockwise	Trust in my perceptions.	Clockwise	Neither trust my senses nor *what* I see.
Throat	Clockwise	Feeling free to express myself.	Counter-Clockwise	Fear to express myself.
Heart	Counter-Clockwise	Sense of serving a (good) purpose. "I love, am loved, and have so much to give."	Clockwise	Sense that I and life have no (good) purpose. "I am hurt and unloved. I am running on empty."
Solar Plexus	Clockwise	Agreeing with life in general.	Counter-Clockwise	Sense of hopeless-ness and powerless-ness. Not seeing any options and, there-fore, disagreeing with life in general.
Sacral	Couinter-Clockwise	Feeling free to create. Activities are joyous and rewarding.	Clockwise	Not enjoying one's activities, yet feeling paralyzed, constricted and stifled to do anything else.
Base	Clockwise	Feeling safe and supported in general.	Counter-Clockwise	Feeling vastly unpro-tected, in the face of constant threats and dangers.

Table 3: Effect of Attitudes on Chakra Rotation

coupled with the Ego (please compare Fig. 6b with Fig. 4). The Ego, if it is also mainly located on that side, will literally *drive* or *pull* consciousness and attitudes in general (the total Mind) in a counter-clockwise direction, as indicated by the large arrow in Fig. 6b. Unfortunately, this rotation appears *ego-syntonic*. It is reflective of and supported by our prevalent cultural values and strivings. Therefore, it probably feels good and right to the individual. Perhaps it is the mindset downright *required* by our circumstances in order to continue doing what we are doing, i.e., in order to maintain those circumstances. We have long started to *serve the machine* we once invented, while continuing to perfect that machine (the Humanoid), all the while living in fear of eventually losing control over our own invention.

> Is it this rotation—of too many individuals, in their respective communities, countries and in the world who, by means of materialism, squeeze the spirit out of everything they touch—that causes the earth to *wobble* around the sun? Is it that we resist vibrating in the inherently harmonious frequency of the universe, proud, joyous and erect, full of spirit—*fully* ALIVE?!
>
> In his book, *Wherever you go, there you are* (1994), Jon Kabat-Zinn tells of his difficulty to convey the concept of low self-esteem to the Dalai Lama. "...So many people in America carry deep feelings of self-loathing and inadequacy," while "Such feelings are virtually unheard of among the Tibetans [at least from the *male* perspective; it would be interesting to hear from some of the women]. ...Maybe we are overdeveloped outwardly and underdeveloped inwardly. Perhaps it is we who, for all our wealth are living in poverty."

While this may sound harsh, it *is* good food for thought. It is always a good idea to *self-scrutinize,* instead of waiting to *be criticized.* America has been on an output mode for a long time. When we finally consider that we may have become internally impoverished for our outward focus, there may be no other, vastly different cultural values left from which to learn, from which to take in. Unfortunately, if we now find ourselves lacking something as a result of our strivings (e.g., good health and well-being), we also know that we inadvertently spread this void, too, along with spreading our hallmarks of civilization, just as we brought measles, alcoholism and many other diseases to Native Americans. A balancing act of Yin/Yang will, inevitably, force us to balance our input/output modes (*active listening* instead of *aggressive marketing*) in the world, as within our own country.

Therefore, before such a major balancing act can occur, perhaps we first have to ask ourselves, just how seriously we really *want* to heal, ourselves and each other. We are all in both roles, healer and helee, some of the time, as patients, doctors, teachers, mothers, spouses, friends and ministers. "How do *I* heal and what do I need most (but rarely receive) in order to heal" and, "Am I really willing and ready to go the distance in order to heal"? Like the alcoholic, we must ask ourselves, "Have I/we reached bottom yet"? Bridging the helping models is a questions of responsibility, consciousness, purpose and motivation. Our health care crisis is but one symptom of our individual and collective distress, as subjectively experienced but not attended to. The logical physical manifestation of all ignored distress is, indeed, always a *crisis*, e.g., an urgent, debilitating illness, a marital break-up, a revolution or anything which can suddenly no longer be ignored. Let us forget about money, power, exclusive domains and *mine versus yours* for a moment and reflect upon where we truly want to go and what would be a good solution for you *and* me. When purpose and motivation are right—i.e., in agreement with divine will and harmony—the means *will* follow. Such is the order of God. Such is the order of the universe. It is my sincere hope that this book will contribute to solving the "Urgent Dilemma" concerning the needed paradigm and modality definitions which the European Council 1994 called for (Jonas, W.B., 1995), by providing one congruent frame work, format and language for such definitions. All—framework/paradigm and the resulting definitions—will reflect our consciousness and purpose *today*. Further, they will give us a *direction for tomorrow,* for creating the legal, political and professional environments in which Holism can flourish. Let us make this a "Yes" to life—a clockwise, life-promoting direction, conducive for unfolding *more* of what there is to life.

The very best of health and life to all!

REFERENCES

Armstrong, M. & Pettigrew, M. (Producers), & Read, D. (Director). (1993). *The burning times* [Film]. Santa Monica, CA: Direct Cinema Limited.

Bach, E. & Wheeler, F.J. (1977). *The Bach Flower Remedies*. New Canaan, CT: Keats Publishing.

Baumol, W.J. & Blinder, A.S. (1986). *Economics: Principles and policy.* New York, NY: Harcourt Brace Jovanovich.

Benor, D.J. (1991, Summer). *Psi healing research.* ISSSEEM Newsletter, pp. 11-12.

Bradshaw, J. (1988). *Healing the shame that binds you.* Deerfield Beach, FL: Health Communications.

Brennan, B.A. (1993). *Light emerging*. New York, NY: Bantam Books.

Califano, Jr., J.A. (1994). *Radical surgery: What's next for America's health care.* New York, NY: Random House.

Carlson, R. & Shield, B. (Eds.). (1989). *Healers on healing*. New York, NY: Tarcher/Putnam.

Colburn, D. (1995, November 22). U.S. hospitals' way of death resists change. *The Washington Post,* pp. A1, A10.

Corsini, R.J. & Wedding, D. (1989). *Current psychotherapies.* Itasca, IL: Peacock.

Dahlke, R. (1992). *Krankheit als Sprache der Seele* [translation: *Illness—Language of the Soul*]. Munich, Germany: Bertelsmann.

Dailey, W.H. (1994, Fall). Piecing the puzzle together: Evolving a new health paradigm. *Bridges,* pp. 10-12.

Davidson, J. (1987). *Subtle energy.* Saffron Walden, England: C.W. Daniel.

Dethlefsen, T. & Dahlke, R. (1983). *The healing power of illness: The meaning of symptoms and how to interpret them.* Rockport, MA: Element.

Eabry, S. (1994, Jan/Feb). Beware the robes of science. *Massage,* 47.

Fahrion, S.L., Wirkus, M., & Pooley, P. (1992). EEG amplitude, brain mapping, & synchrony in & between a bioenergy practitioner & client during healing. *Subtle Energies,* **3**, 1, 19-52.

Fox, M. (Speaker). (1994). *Sacred work/sacred service* (Cassette Recording No. BSD-16). Boston, MA: Body & Soul New Age Journal & Interface.

Green, E. (1993). Mind over matter: Volition and the cosmic connection in Yogic theory. *Subtle Energies*, **4**, 2, 151-170.

Green, E. (1994, Fall). The necessity for promoting health: Or, as they might say in Washington, it's health, stupid, not sickness. *Bridges*, pp. 1, 4, 5.

Green, E.E., Parks, P.A., Guyer, P.M., Fahrion, S.L. & Coyne, L. (1991). Anomalous electrostatic phenomena in exceptional subjects. *Subtle Energies*, **2**, 3, 69-94.

Grossinger, R. (1995, Winter). Beyond the ideology of healing. *Gnosis*, pp. 51-56.

Harman, W.W. (1995, Summer). What kind of science. *Bridges*, pp. 1, & 8-11.

Harvey, G. & Hardman, C. (Eds.). (1996). *Paganism today*. San Francisco, CA: Harper Collins.

Hay, L.L. (1982). *Heal your body: The mental causes for physical illness and the metaphysical way to overcome them*. Santa Monica, CA: Hay House.

Herman, R. (1995, August 1). Therapies outside the mainstream. *The Washington Post*, pp. A1, A6.

Horst, E.A. (1996, July). Patriarchy: An experiential definition. *The ISTI Sun*, **2**, 3, pp. 1, 2, & 4.

Jaroff, L. (1994, November). A no-touch therapy. *Time*, p. 76.

Jessel-Kenyon, J. (Speaker). (1994). *Subtle Energy Detection & Measurements*. (Cassette Recording No. ISD-4). Boulder, CO: 4th Annual International Society for the Study of Subtle Energies & Energy Medicine Conference.

Jonas, W.B. (1995, August 29). Complementary, alternative & unconventional medicine. *Complementary medicine seminar series*. Conducted by the Uniformed Services University of the Health Sciences (USUHS), in cooperation with the National Institutes of Health, in Washington, D.C.

Kabat-Zinn, J. (1994). *Wherever you go, there you are*. New York, NY: Hyperion.

Karagulla, S. & Van Gelder Kunz, D. (1989). *The Chakras and the human energy fields*. Wheaton, IL: The Theosophical Publishing House.

Krippner, S. (1994, Spring). "Energy Medicine" in Native American healing practices. *Bridges*, pp. 1, 7.

Leadbeater, C.W. (1925). *Man visible and invisible.* Wheaton, IL: The Theosophical Publishing House.

Leadbeater, C.W. & Besant, A. (1933). *Thought-forms*. Wheaton, IL: The Theosophical Publishing House.

McDowell, B. (1994, October). [Interview with Andrew Weil, Center for Integrative Medicine, Tucson, AZ]. Championing integrative medicine. *Alternative & Complementary Therapies*, **1**, 1, pp. 8-13.

Miller, Jr., G.T. (1979). *Living in the environment: An introduction to environmental science*. Belmont, CA: Wadsworth.

Moyers, B. (1993). *Healing and the mind.* New York, NY: Bantam Doubleday Dell.

Pavek, R.R. & Trachtenberg, A.I. (1995). Current status of alternative health practices in the United States. *Contemporary Internal Medicine*, **7**, 8, 61-71.

Redwood, D. (1995, Summer). [Interview with Marc Micozzi, Director of the National Museum of Health and Medicine]. Merging mainstream medicine with alternative therapies can ease the health care crisis. *Pathways*, pp. 11, 13, & 100-104.

Rein, G. (Speaker). (1994). (Cassette Recording No. ISD-4). Boulder, CO: 4th Annual International Society for the Study of Subtle Energies & Energy Medicine Conference.

Schneider, C.J. (1994). *A letter from the president.* (Available from The International Society for the Study of Subtle Energies & Energy Medicine, 356 Goldco Circle, Golden, CO 80403).

Sessions Stepp, L. (1996, February 5). A wonder drug's worst side effect: Ritalin, the newest available cheap high. *The Washington Post*, pp. A1, A6.

Srinivasan, T.M. (1993). The paradox of holism. *Subtle Energies*, **4**, 3, 215-230.

St. George, D. (1994). Research into complementary medicine. *Advances*, **10**, 3, pp. 59-60.

Stanford, R. (1987). *Fatima prophecy.* New York, NY: Ballantine Books.

Stearn, J. (1967). *Edgar Cayce: The sleeping prophet.* New York, NY: Bantam Books.

Strieber, W. (1988). *Transformation: The breakthrough.* New York, NY: Beech Tree Books.

Stolz, A. (1988). Schamanen [translation: Shamanism]. Koeln, Germany: Du Mont.

Sylvest, V.M. (Speaker). (1992). *Who gets sick or well and why?* (Cassette Recording). Richmond, VA: The Institute of Higher Learning.

The Burton Goldberg Group (1993). *Alternative medicine: The definitive guide.* Puyallup, WA: Future Medicine Publishing.

The Fason Foundation Charitable Trust (1995, Spring). $930,000,000.00 at stake. *You may never be sick again,* p.1.

Thompson, K. (1996, Summer). Coming ashore to a larger earth. *Noetic Sciences Review,* pp. 4-11, & 34-37.

Walsh, P. (Producer & Director). (1992). *Bioenergy: A healing art* [Film]. Bethesda, MD: Wirkus Bioenergy Foundation.

Watts, Alan (1961). *Psychotherapy East and West.* New York, NY: Vintage Books.

White, J. (1987). Consciousness and substance: The primal forms of God. *Journal of Near-Death-Studies,* **6**, 2, 73-78.

APPENDIX: Nomenclature

TERM	DESCRIPTION	SYNONYM	DISTINGUISHED FROM
ALLOPATHIC MEDICINE	Standard western model. Viewing & treating disease as "pathology" and as distinctly different or even opposite from "health."	"Traditional" Medicine	Homeopathy; Holistic Health
ALTERNATIVE MEDICINE	Methods adopted from models other than the standard western one for medicine, usually as body-centered therapies. When integrated into the allopathic framework, the philosophical context of many of these therapies is lost and, with it, a large part of their effectiveness.	Complementary Medicine	
ASTRAL PLANE	Feeling realm. The plane of existence which is energetically denser than the thinking realm (Mental), but more subtle than the physical (incl. the ether) realm.	Astral Body = Emotional Body	
ATTITUDE(S)	Astral & Mental energy construct(s), conscious or unconscious. "An attitude about something" is a particular feeling-thinking complex or syndrome, elicited by a certain stimulus. Disharmonious attitudes eventually affect and involve Causal elements on the Causal plane.		

TERM	DESCRIPTION	SYNONYM	DISTINGUISHED FROM
AURA	Used loosely to describe *any* subtle energy body/field a person may be able to perceive. Mostly, this refers to the etheric field.	Corona; Non-specific Energy Field/Body	
BASE CHAKRA	Energy/force center located at the base of the spine.	Root Chakra	
BIO-ENERGY	All subtle energies—without differentiating between different energy density—which are produced and/or maintained by one and the same organism. The organism's *own* subtle energies.		Artificially generated energies
BODY-(CENTERED) THERAPIES	Any therapy that specifically aims at effecting changes in or to the physical body, either within a holistic, allopathic or homeopathic context.		Spiritual Therapies; Psychotherapies
BOUNDARIES	Used in psychology to designate emotional and mental (=attitudinal) limit-setting, in a conscious, deliberate fashion. Purpose of boundaries is to distinguish oneself from others, to maintain individual integrity and to protect self from abuse by others.		
BROW CHAKRA	Energy/force center located in the middle of the forehead. Seat of spirit will.	"Third Eye"	

TERM	DESCRIPTION	SYNONYM	DISTINGUISHED FROM
CHAKRA(S) (SANSKRIT: "WHEEL")	Energy "whirlpools" of iridescent light/colors, which are the "organs" of our subtle energy bodies. The seven main Chakras represent our non-physical (spiritual) sensory organs and "communicators."	Force Center(s); Energy Center(s)	
CAUSAL PLANE	Energetically finest, most subtle of all planes of existence beneath the heavens. Realm of abstract intent, goals and purpose. "Blue Print" for the Mind.	Causal Body = "Higher Self"	
CROWN CHAKRA	Energy/force center located on the top of the head.		
DISTANT (SUBTLE ENERGY) THERAPY	Therapy "sent" through subtle energy realms from a practitioner to a person who is physically located elsewhere. This activity follows the same principles as prayer, i.e., on subtle energy realms, *thinking is doing*. Usually, it is more specific than prayer and involves both, the sending *and* receiving of information/stimuli.	Remote Therapy; Non-local Therapy	Hands-On Therapy
EGO	A construct of feelings, thoughts and goals, arbitrarily selected from all our (and sometimes others') subtle energy bodies. This construct serves as an *assumed self*, as long as we are vastly unconscious of our true Mind or being	Assumed Self	

TERM	DESCRIPTION	SYNONYM	DISTINGUISHED FROM
EMBODIED (SELF)	A spirit which has assumed form by "clothing" itself with energy substance from each plane of existence (the "clothing" represents the Soul), with or without necessarily choosing a physical incarnation. Commonly, however, "embodied" refers to a spirit-soul complex which has assumed *physical* form, usually as a human being.	Incarnated	Dis-embodied; Discarnate
(SUBTLE) ENERGY FIELD/BODY	Energetic (non-physical) "clouds," permeating and surrounding all organisms and objects. Their energies are finer (more subtle) than most measurable ones at this time.	Plane/Realm of Existence	Physical Body; Matter
ETHER BODY OR ETHERIC FIELD	Subtle energy field following the contours of the physical body, extending but an inch or so beyond the physical skin. Energetically the most subtle of the seven *physical* realms. "Blue Print" for matter, including all flesh. Dissolves upon physical death. *Adj.* etheric.	"Etheric Double"; Vital Body; "Aura"	
HEART CHAKRA	Energy/force center located in the area of the heart (chest). Seat of intuition.		

TERM	DESCRIPTION	SYNONYM	DISTINGUISHED FROM
HEALER	Health practitioner. Although any reference to healing is owned by the medical establishment, "healer" usually denotes a practitioner ascribing to a model *other* than the conventional one.		
HEALING	The restoration of (divine) harmony in the Body-Mind-Spirit, as well as in the environment, by allowing the spirit to lead.		Harming
HOLISM	A philosophy or paradigm placing *spirit* at center stage. All of creation is run *by* spirit, *for* spirit. All of life has one purpose, i.e., to allow the inherent spirit to take the reigns, by voluntarily subordinating all other, less evolved (or energetically denser) components. In health care, holism refers to the role of illness as a teaching mechanism in this learning process, i.e., redemption of body and Mind *through* spirit. Holistic health care, therefore, involves attending to the (physical) body, Mind and spirit, as well as environmental considerations, for optimal learning conditions and results.	The "Body-Mind-Spirit" (and the Environment)	Reductionism
HOLISTIC THERAPY	Any healing art based on holism.	Holistic "Modality"	Conventional Therapy

TERM	DESCRIPTION	SYNONYM	DISTINGUISHED FROM
KARMA	*Spiritual* law of cause & effect: A self-regulating law of ultimate justice (not to be confused with "punishment"), whereby the spirit chooses its own, best conditions for unlearning previous errors.	"Fate"; "Kismet"	Law of physics concerning *physical* cause-and-effect relationships.
KIRLIAN PHOTO-GRAPHY	A special photographic process that makes the etheric field and its vitality visible. Typically used to photograph the ether aura around fingertips and toes. Comes with a topography relating the photographed areas to every part of the physical body. Helpful to diagnose impending or already physically manifested illness, based on lack of vitality in certain ether-body areas.		
KUNDALINI	Two kinds of energy of opposite charge or polarization (some writings mention a third, neutral life force), curving around the full length of the spine, thus connecting the seven main Chakras and driving their rotation. From the earth below, through the Base Chakra, Kundalini is nourished with the feminine component, and with masculine (opposite charge) energy from above, through the Crown.	"Life Force"; "Serpent Fire"	

TERM	DESCRIPTION	SYNONYM	DISTINGUISHED FROM
MENTAL PLANE	Thinking realm. The plane of existence which is energetically denser than the Causal plane, yet more subtle than the feeling realm (Astral plane).		
MIND	The sum of all subtle energy bodies (excluding the etheric field, which is part of the physical realm) and all their content—feeling, thinking and purpose/goals/motivation, conscious and unconscious.	Soul; Psyche; Personality; the "I" or "Self"	Common mind, referring to conscious awareness only; "Universal Mind," usually depicting purest spirit, the voice of God or content of "the heavens"
MODALITY (HOLISTIC)		SEE: Hol. Therapy	
PARADIGM	Philosophy or world view attempting to conceptualize all that is, in a systematic, orderly fashion. Paradigms need be expanded or discarded in the face of phenomena and new discoveries which cannot be explained by the prevailing world view. Examples of previous world views which were eventually abandoned: The earth being flat or all planets' revolving around the earth.		*Model(s) for specific applications,* e.g., health, science and religion. However, every paradigm shift usually affects these models.
PERSONALITY		SEE: Mind	
PSYCHE		SEE: Mind	
REMOTE THERAPY		SEE: Distant Therapy	

TERM	DESCRIPTION	SYNONYM	DISTINGUISHED FROM
ROOT CHAKRA		SEE: Base Chakra	
SACRAL CHAKRA	Energy/force center located in the middle of the lower abdomen.	Sexual Chakra	
SOLAR PLEXUS	Energy/force center located slightly above the navel. Seat of the ego.		
SOUL		SEE: Mind	Spirit (purest, original form of energy or consciousness)
SPIRITUAL THERAPY	All therapies attempting to produce an effect in any of the subtle energy (non-physical, hence "spiritual") bodies. Being the physical blueprint, work on the ether/vital body is, by definition, a Body Therapy. Indeed, related therapies usually intend to effect changes in the *physical* body.		Body-(Centered) Therapy
SUBTLE ENERGY	Energies that comprise all feeling and thinking, plus those of much higher functioning, e.g., intuiting, spirit will, purpose, intent, love, insight (Eureka experiences), healing, all so-called "psychic" abilities/perceptions, consciousness and life itself.	"Pranas" (Ayurvedic)	
VITAL BODY		SEE: Ether Body or Etheric Field	

About the Author

Photo by Benjamin Ritter

Lilo Bauer-Freitag is a conventional psychotherapist who has ventured into the fields of subtle energy dynamics and phytotherapy. She is now a practicing consultant and an ordained minister in Northern Virginia advising on holistic living and subtle energy techniques. She was trained and initiated into the art of Bio-Energy in Saarbruecken, Germany, by Ursula Philippi, a Licensed Naturopathic Practitioner. As a so-called "sensitive" and "medical intuitive," Lilo incorporates a variety of skills into her repertoire, such as classical Chakra and Regression Therapy, and using the subtle energy properties of herbs and flower essences.

While a holistic advocate, Lilo is keenly familiar with scientific conventions and is also equipped with feminine "memory," intuition and the resulting skills. She is devoted to stimulating and streamlining cooperation in the scientific, professional, legal and political environment for holism in America. Her efforts include the coining of a common language across the disciplines, to define the holistic world view (or "paradigm") and the integration of all health care into one.

Lilo's academic training includes:

- Master of Arts in Clinical Counseling (Oakland University. Rochester, Michigan)
- Bachelor of Arts in Divinity (Universal Brotherhood University. Norcross, Georgia)
- Bachelor of Arts in Psychology (University of Maryland, European Division)

Here's how to order additional copies of

Healing: The Emerging Holistic Paradigm

by L. Bauer-Freitag

Please send \$16.00 per copy + \$3.50 shipping for 1st copy; add \$1.00 shipping for each additional copy to the same address. Books are shipped by 1st class mail.

Your Name (please print) ______________________________

Address to send book(s) ______________________________

____

____

No. of copies ordered__________ Amount enclosed__________

Please make checks payable to and send orders to

Lilo Bauer-Freitag
P.O. Box 41927
Fredericksburg, VA
22404